MW01060033

PRESENTED TO:

Kassidy

FROM:

Grandma + Grandpa

DATE:

May 14, 2010

God's Little
Devotional Book
for Girls

God's Little Devotional Book

 for Girls

David C Cook
transforming lives together

GOD'S LITTLE DEVOTIONAL BOOK FOR GIRLS
Published by David C. Cook
4050 Lee Vance View
Colorado Springs, CO 80918 U.S.A.

David C. Cook Distribution Canada
55 Woodslee Avenue, Paris, Ontario, Canada N3L 3E5

David C. Cook U.K., Kingsway Communications
Eastbourne, East Sussex BN23 6NT, England

David C. Cook and the graphic circle C logo
are registered trademarks of Cook Communications Ministries.

ISBN 978-1-56292-206-1

© 2004 by Bordon Books

Manuscript written by W. B. Freeman

Printed in the United States of America
First Edition 2004

14 15 16 17 18 19 20 21 22 23

100509

INTRODUCTION

Who can find a virtuous—honest, worthy, and pure—woman? Her price is far above rubies (see Proverbs 31:10 KJV). "How did she become a virtuous woman?" you ask. Her parents and those who love her soaked her in God's love and goodness since she was your age or younger. This wonderful devotional book is filled with fun stories, powerful scriptures, and guiding life principles written to help a young woman just like you become all that God wants her to be.

You will experience God's presence and guidance through the stories about girls your own age. You can learn life-changing, spiritual principles on faith, friendship, kindness, and many other Christian values. Find out how much God loves you. Understand that in His eyes you are beautiful, and that beauty and godliness go together.

With *God's Little Devotional Book for Girls*, you can take a quiet break from school and extracurricular activities and discover the God who loves you, knows you, and wants you to become all you were created by Him to be.

She Said

God is everywhere! The God who framed humankind to be one mighty family, himself our Father, and the world our home.

Erica walked slowly into the kitchen. Her mother noticed her worried look. "Erica, is something wrong?"

Erica didn't answer. She was trying to figure out what she had done to make Emily walk off in tears. And Samantha and Shay had both had puzzled looks on their faces when they left the front yard.

"Mom, Emily ran away crying. I don't know why she was so sad. We were just playing and talking...."

"What were you talking about?" her mother asked.

"Sammy was talking about how her daddy was a policeman and he put bad people in jail. Shay said her daddy was an insurance agent and arranged to have people's roofs fixed when it hailed. I said my daddy climbed telephone poles. We waited for Emily to say what her daddy did, but she just started crying and ran home."

Erica's mom poured a glass of juice for Erica and sat down at the table. Erica sat down next to her. "Honey, Emily's daddy doesn't live with her. I don't know where he lives, and Emily doesn't remember him."

"Oh," Erica said. "I didn't know."

Her mother continued, "It's okay to talk about your daddy. You just need to be sensitive to others' feelings. Emily probably just didn't know what to say since she doesn't know what her daddy does."

"Oh." Erica thought about that while she finished her juice. "Mom, I think I should go over to Emily's and ask her what her mommy does and tell her it's okay if her daddy doesn't live with her because God is her Heavenly Daddy. Right?"

"That would be a nice thing to do," her mother said. "I'll go with you."

We have one Father—God.
John 8:41 NKJV

GOD IS YOUR LOVING FATHER.

You may have a wonderful father here on earth, but remember to think about God as your Father too. Thank him for making you part of his great family.

Lunch?

Good to forgive, best to forget.

Kaylyn walked slowly to the lunchroom, silently praying *God, please don't let me have to sit alone again.* She had sat alone for three weeks now—because of Ashley. She had always had lots of friends until Ashley told everyone that Kaylyn had cheated on a test. It wasn't true, and even the teacher said that Kaylyn didn't cheat. But that wasn't enough for Ashley. She kept saying terrible things about Kaylyn. Kaylyn got in line.

"Kaylyn?" Kaylyn turned to see Ashley standing behind her. Shocked, and trying to control her anger, Kaylyn looked at her.

Ashley took a deep, shaky breath and said, "I'm really sorry for starting the rumor that you cheated on the test."

"I appreciate that, Ashley, but what made you say something like that? I thought we were friends."

Ashley moved her tray behind Kaylyn's. "We are friends, but I was really jealous of you. You always make such good grades, and everything seems to be so easy for you. I always have to work really hard—and my grades aren't good at all."

"But, Ashley, my grades don't come easy. I have to study really hard too. Maybe we could study together for the next test—so we can both get the grades we want."

"You mean that? You would study with me after what I said?"

"What you did really hurt, but I forgive you."

Ashley sighed with relief. "Thanks," she whispered. "I still want to be friends."

"Me too," Kaylyn said. She and Ashley walked happily to the lunch table to eat with all their friends.

Forgive as the Lord forgave you.
Colossians 3:13 NIV

IF SOMEONE ASKS, FORGIVE THEM.

Do you have a friend you need to forgive? Ask God for help; then with his help, forgive them.

A Leash and a Fence

Nothing can be done without hope
and confidence.

— ✳ —

"What's wrong?" Andi asked. It wasn't very often that she saw her tough little sister, Alyson, cry.

"It's that big, old bulldog Bart, down the street. He's mean."

"Let's go see," Andi said. Alyson wasn't all that interested in taking another look at Bart, but she took her sister's hand and they walked down to Bart's yard. As if on cue, Bart lunged against his leash and began to bark ferociously. Andi could see why Alyson was scared. Bart bared his teeth when he barked and he looked as if he wanted to eat them alive.

Andi thought for a moment and said, "Aly, let's just stand here a minute."

"I'd rather go home," Alyson said through her tears.

"No," Andi said and hung tightly to her sister's hand. "Don't look at Bart. Look at the leash. See how strong it is. It's tied to a big metal stake. Now look at this chain-link fence. It's strong and it's too high for Bart to get over." Alyson looked and nodded.

"Do you remember what Grandpa taught us last summer out at the farm about the big bull that looked so mean?"

"Yeah," Alyson said. "He said it was like the Devil. Grandpa said we shouldn't look at the Devil or listen to him. God has the Devil leashed up and fenced in."

"That's right. And the same thing is true for Bart."

The two girls were so busy talking about Grandpa, the fence, and the leash that they almost missed the fact that Bart the bull-dog had grown tired of barking and was lying down in the grass, chewing a bone. When the girls finally saw what he was doing, Alyson started to giggle. "Ol' Bart's already got something to chew!" she said.

The devil prowls around like a roaring lion ...
But resist him, firm in *your* faith.
1 Peter 5:8–9 NASB

TRUST GOD TO HELP YOU.

God has given you faith to trust him. Believe he will protect you from all harm! Put your hope and confidence in him.

Dress Up's on the Way

Everyone is a potential winner, even though some people are disguised as losers. Don't let their appearance fool you.

"Oh, no," Lisa groaned. "Margo's coming ... and she's pulling her little red wagon behind her."

"Oh, dear," Mom said. "Is her red wagon piled high with dress-up clothing?"

"Yes," Lisa said. "I hate playing dress up. I'd rather climb a tree."

"I know," Mom said. "But Margo is a really nice girl. She's a good friend."

"Most of the time," said Lisa. "I'm not sure she's such a good friend when she wants to play something I don't like to play."

"I know something you like to do," Mom said. "It's something that might make an afternoon with Margo go by a little faster."

"What?" Lisa said. "You'd better hurry and tell me because she's almost here."

"You like to make up stories. Tell Margo that you'll play dress up with her if she'll let you make up a play first. Then you can each pick out a costume to wear while you recite your lines."

Lisa jumped at the idea. She really did like making up stories and writing them into little plays. When Margo got to her house, Lisa told her the plan. Margo thought it was a good idea and the two girls went to work immediately, making up characters and writing a little play on Lisa's computer. In fact, they got so busy that two hours went by before Margo's mother called to ask Margo to come home. They never got around to trying on any of the clothes in Margo's red wagon.

After Margo left, Mom asked, "Well, how did it go?"

Lisa grinned and said, "Great! Margo's coming back tomorrow afternoon."

"Will you be playing dress up then?" Mom asked.

"No!" said Lisa with an even bigger grin. "We'll be rehearsing. There's a huge difference!"

Always seek after that which is good for one another.
1 Thessalonians 5:15 NASB

CREATING TOGETHER IS FUN.

When you make a decision to create something good with another person, you can usually find something you both enjoy doing. Ask God to show you how to have a win-win time with your friends.

Look Up and Out!

When the world is spinning, look up!

"Are you sure you want to go on this ride?"

Janette had been sure when her father asked her, but now as she was about to step into the two-person basket on her first Ferris wheel ride, she wondered if she had made the right choice. The Ferris wheel had looked a lot smaller when she stood at the entrance to the fairgrounds. Janette was grateful that her father was by her side.

As the Ferris wheel began to move and she found herself rising higher and higher, she was excited. "I don't think I've ever been so high up in all my life! Mom and Noah look really small!"

Then the Ferris wheel crested and their basket began to move downward. Janette's stomach seemed to flip over and she thought she might get sick. "Ohhhh," she moaned.

"Are you okay?" Dad asked.

"Yes," she said, swallowing hard.

The Ferris wheel made another turn and then, to Janette's surprise, it stopped. Their basket was just barely starting down from the top. It swung there, high above the ground.

"We're really high, Dad," she said, barely above a whisper.

"I know," he said. "It's best not to look down. Look up and look out. Look up at the stars and look out at the city lights in the distance. You can see downtown!" Dad went on, "If you look up and look out, you won't feel dizzy or sick."

Dad's idea worked! Later, when the ride was over and they ate hot dogs, Janette told her mother about looking up and looking out. "The same thing is true for all of life," Mom said. "If you feel a little nervous, look up to God! Look at the future he has planned ahead of you!"

Depend on the Lord. Trust him, and
he will take care of you.
Psalm 37:5 ICB

ALWAYS LOOK TO GOD.

Don't get discouraged or afraid of what you see around you. Look to God and trust him to lead you. Pray, "God, help me! Protect me! Prepare me for the good things You have in store for me!"

17

A Shower of Kindness

Be kind to unkind people—they need it most.

Hannah felt that Nelda was the meanest person she had ever met. If anybody was going to cut into line … push someone away from the drinking fountain … or start a bad rumor … it would be Nelda.

"She goes out of her way to be mean," Hannah said to her friends Lucy and Gillian.

"I agree," Lucy said, "but if we do mean things to her, we're no better than she is."

Gillian added, "She'd probably just get meaner."

"Well, then," Hannah said, "it's obvious! We'll shower her with kindness."

"That will be hard," Lucy gulped.

"Very hard," Gillian said, "but I'm willing to try."

For the next three days, the girls invited Nelda to sit with them on the bus. They didn't say anything when she interrupted or pushed her way ahead of them. Nelda didn't seem to notice.

Then, on the fourth day, Nelda fell while rushing to get to the auditorium for the assembly. She scraped her knee badly. The three girls stopped to help her. "I don't need your help," Nelda said, holding her bleeding knee.

"Here's my headband to stop the blood from getting on your clothes," Hannah said as she pulled off her cloth headband and handed it to Nelda. "I'll go with you to get a bandage," she said, helping Nelda to her feet.

"We won't get good seats," Nelda said.

"Gillian and I will save two seats on the aisle," Lucy said.

"We'd like to be your friends," Hannah said as she walked with Nelda to the nurse's office.

"But why?" Nelda said. "I'm mean to you." Nelda was quiet for a few seconds and then said, "Thanks. I'd like to be your friend, too."

It was the nicest thing Hannah had ever heard her say!

By our purity, knowledge, patience, and kindness
we have shown ourselves to be God's servants.
2 Corinthians 6:6 TEV

KIND WORDS PRODUCE KINDNESS!

When you continue to show kindness to someone mean, there is a good chance your kindness will rub off on them.

The Dollhouse

With time and patience the mulberry leaf
becomes silk.

Casandra and Mari had worked on the dollhouse for three weeks. "It still doesn't look like a house," Casandra sighed.

"I know," Mari said. "But we do have all the wallpaper on the inside wall pieces, and the floor and ceiling pieces are made." Casandra added, "So are the windows and curtains."

"I've really been wondering, though, if we'll get it finished in time for the Christmas party," Casandra said.

"We have to," Mari said. "It's our present!"

"We might be able to buy something else," Casandra said. "Not anything this nice, but at least something."

"No," Mari said. "Remember? We talked about it and we even prayed about it. We asked God to help us think of a really great gift to give to the girls' group home, and right after that we thought about making a dollhouse for the little girls who live there. We already have lots of furniture from our old dollhouses and from the thrift stores we've been to. We can't quit now! We just need to ask God to help us work faster."

"I know God will help us," Casandra said. "We just can't make any mistakes. We have to work as fast as we can and, at the same time, work slowly enough to do a good job."

"Right!" Mari said. "If we don't give up, we'll get it done."

When the girls presented their dollhouse at the group home two weeks later, everybody oohed and aahed. "When did you find time to make it?" the home leader asked.

"After school and on Saturdays," Mari said.

Casandra added, "It was a God job! We did the work, and he gave us the idea and helped us all the way. And mostly God helped me not to give up."

No one can please God without faith, for whoever comes to God must have faith that God exists and rewards those who seek him.
Hebrews 11:6 TEV

GOD'S HELP IS THE BEST HELP!

Trust God to help you do your best and to get your work done on time with diligence.

Making the Team

Prayer does not cause faith to work; faith
causes prayer to work.

Belinda took gymnastics classes for a full year before she finally felt that she might be ready to try out for her school's gymnastics team. "I've been praying and praying, but I'm still not sure God is going to answer my prayers that I will make the team," Belinda said to her mother.

"Do you believe God will help you if you make the team?" her mother asked.

"Sure!" Belinda said. "God helps me all the time."

"Do you believe God will help you if you don't make the team?" her mother then asked.

Belinda was puzzled. "What would there be for him to help me do if I didn't make the team?"

"Oh, lots of things," her mother said. "You'd need to keep smiling and keep having a positive attitude. You'd need to keep trying and doing your best in gymnastics class. Those seem like pretty hard things to do if you don't make the team."

"They sure would be," Belinda said. "I don't think I could pretend that it didn't matter. Everybody knows how much I want to make the team. So I'd have to be willing to admit that I was hurt and disappointed."

"That's sometimes the most difficult thing to do," her mother said. "But do you think God would help you in all of that?"

"Yes," said Belinda. "I believe God can help me do all things—the things I want to do that are hard, and the things I don't want to do."

"That's real faith," her mother said. "That's the kind of faith that will help you pray, 'Do what is best in my life, God—even if it isn't always what I want.'"

Remember

There is nothing that God cannot do.
Luke 1:37 TEV

GOD SPECIALIZES IN MIRACLES.

You Can Do It!

It is hard to admit that you are hurting, you have failed, or you have made a mistake. Even so, telling God about your hurts and failures is the first step toward trusting God to heal you, forgive you, or help you.

Blowing Up!

No matter how just your words may be, you
ruin everything when you speak with anger.

"I really let 'em have it," Laurie said as she sat down at the dinner table.

"I see," Dad said. "Let's thank God for the food and then you can tell us *what* you let *who* have."

Over dinner, Laurie told her parents and sister how she had listened to a class debate about whether God was real and whether God had created the world like the Bible said he did.

"I kept trying to speak but nobody would let me talk," Laurie said. "So right before the bell rang, I stood up and told them all that if they didn't believe in God and the Bible, they were going to hell."

"Hmmm." Laurie's father and mother looked at each other in silence. "That was pretty radical," her older sister said. Laurie didn't understand why they didn't applaud what she had done.

"Do you believe you changed anybody's mind by saying that?" Dad finally asked. "Probably not," Laurie admitted. "But I feel better."

"Do you really?" Mom asked. "You might feel better for a couple of hours because you let off some steam, but when you go

to school on Monday, will you feel better?" Laurie hadn't tho
about that.

That night she had trouble going to sleep. *What am I going to do on Monday?* she kept thinking. On Saturday morning she asked her parents for their advice. "I think you need to tell the class that you're sorry you became so angry and that you hope they'll let you give them your ideas and opinions sometime."

"What will I say to convince them?" Laurie asked.

"That's your real homework for life," Dad said with a smile. "Often our actions speak louder than our words. Others see more than they hear."

Remember

Stupid people express their anger openly, but sensible
people are patient and hold it back.
Proverbs 29:11 TEV

ANGRY WORDS NEVER SOLVE

ANYTHING.

You Can Do It!

It is very difficult to persuade someone to do or believe the right thing if you are angry. Ask the Lord to help you give your opinions in a calm, kind, but confident voice.

Keep Skating!

A handful of patience is worth more than a bushel of brains.

Ava's brother Eddie helped her put on her elbow guards, kneepads, and helmet. Ava thought all this safety gear wasn't really necessary, but her parents insisted she wear it if she intended to do any in-line skating.

Once the skates were on, Ava stood in the driveway and held on to Eddie for balance. He helped her to the sidewalk, pulled her hand off his arm, gave her a little push, and said, "Go for it!"

Ava rolled a few feet. This wasn't so bad! The breeze sure felt good. She was sure she'd get the hang of this in no time at all and she could go skating with her friends, and...BAM! Ava suddenly found herself sitting on the sidewalk. *Maybe all this safety gear was a good idea after all,* she thought.

Then she heard Eddie laughing. "Get up and go again!" he said.

With Eddie's help, Ava got up two more times. After her third fall, she was in tears. Inline skating was no fun if all you did was fall. She'd never be any good at this. "I give up!" she sobbed, pulling off her skates.

"You can't give up," Eddie said, sitting down beside her. "Did you notice that each time you tried, you skated a little farther? You just have to be patient. It takes time to learn this stuff."

"You really think I can?" asked Ava, eyeing her brother with a little suspicion.

"Hey, if I can do it, you can too," Eddie said. "Like I told you—be patient. You'll be skating circles around me in no time."

Learn to be patient, so that you will please God
and be given what he has promised.
Hebrews 10:36 CEV

TAKE YOUR TIME AND KEEP TRYING.

Sometimes it takes a while to learn how to do something. Don't quit. Work hard and ask God to help you. He's a great teacher.

Alone with Myself

We are not at peace with others because we are not at peace with ourselves, and we are not at peace with ourselves because we are not at peace with God.

"You've seemed to be upset the last few days," Mom said as she turned out the light for the night. "Can you tell me why, Gabriella?"

"I'm not upset," Gabby said to her mother's silhouette in the doorway. And then, hearing the tone of her own voice, she immediately rolled over, punched her pillow, and snuggled into it.

Mom closed the door. Once she was alone, Gabby began to cry. *I don't know how to tell them about the book,* she thought. Dad had told her he didn't want her taking the book out of the house, not even to show her friends. The book was too expensive and too rare. She could invite her friends inside to see its beautiful paintings, but that was all. Her friends, of course, hadn't wanted to come in, so she had taken the book outside and had spilled her drink on it. Then she smudged it when she tried to mop up the mess. One disaster had turned into another.

"God, please forgive me," Gabby prayed. "I made a big mistake. Please help me."

In the morning, Gabby knew what she needed to do. She took the jar with her unspent allowance money to Dad and told him what she had done and asked him to forgive her. As she reached for the money jar, she realized she felt better than she had felt in days.

Now that we have been put right with God
through faith, we have peace with God
through our Lord Jesus Christ.

Romans 5:1 TEV

GOD'S FORGIVENESS BRINGS FREEDOM.

When you do something that you know breaks one of your parents' rules or God's rules, quickly ask for forgiveness. And then, do what you can to make things right.

A Hard Decision

The best discipline, maybe the only
discipline that really works,
is self-discipline.

Clara stared hard and long at the trays of cookies lying on the dining table. There must have been a hundred of them! She could tell from the sight and the aroma that they were her favorite—pecan, chocolate chip, oatmeal cookies!

Clara looked around. There was no one in sight.

"Who would miss just one cookie from this whole table?" she said aloud to herself.

"Somebody might have counted them out for a special deal," she answered herself, suddenly remembering that Mom was in charge of a big party at school.

"But why did she have to make my favorite? She knew that it would drive me crazy if I saw the cookies here on the table," she said aloud.

"She probably made your favorite because these are for you and your class tomorrow," she replied to herself.

"Nobody will ever know I was the one who took a cookie," she said to herself.

Just at that moment her sister Heather walked into the dining room. "Are you alone?" she asked. "I thought I heard voices arguing."

"Yeah, I'm alone," Clara said, a little embarrassed that her sister had caught her talking to herself.

"What were you arguing with yourself about?" Heather asked.

"Doesn't matter," Clara said as she started to walk out of the dining room.

"Who won the argument?" Heather teased.

"My better self," said Clara. "The me who really wants a cookie but doesn't want to get caught stealing one and the me who is hoping that tomorrow I'll get one anyway. That's who. I've got to get out of here because the smell is driving me crazy!"

The Spirit produces ... self-control.
Galatians 5:22–23 TEV

GOD ALWAYS HELPS YOU.

Do God's will and ask him to give you His power. That will give you real willpower.

A Choice for Love

Where there is hatred, let me sow love.

———— ❋ ————

All of the children began to giggle when the teacher asked the new girl to tell the class her name. She stuttered so badly she couldn't get her first name out for several seconds. When she began to struggle with her last name, the giggling turned into open laughter. The girl—whose name was Brenda—ran from the classroom.

The teacher turned to Sammi, who sat just in front of Brenda and said, "Go after her."

Sammi walked slowly out of the classroom, not at all sure where Brenda went or what to say to her when she found her. Finally, Sammi spotted Brenda sitting in a swing, crying. She walked over to her and said simply, "My name is Sammi, and I will be your friend."

"N-n-n-nobody is my friend," Brenda said.

"Well, I am now," Sammi said. "And I'm going to introduce you to my friends, and then they will be your friends too."

"What m-m-makes you so sure?" Brenda asked with a little less stuttering.

"Because my friends are really nice, once you get to know them. I think you're nice, too, and once they get to know you, you'll fit right in. I can tell." Sammi spoke with a big smile on her face that Brenda couldn't ignore. "Let me prove it to you," Sammi said. "But first, tell me a little about yourself." The two talked for a few minutes and then walked back to the classroom.

When they got to the room, Sammi announced to the entire class, "Our new girl is Brenda Downing. She's from Tennessee and she's got a big brother and a German shepherd and she plays the piano. And she's my friend." Everybody smiled this time … and nobody laughed.

Love one another warmly as Christians.
Romans 12:10 TEV

TO MAKE A NEW FRIEND, BE A FRIEND.

Be willing to make new friends. Reach out with kindness to other children who may be hurting, sad, embarrassed, or lonely.

Café Rules

**You can never go wrong
when you choose to obey Christ.**

The Jacobs family was taking a summer road trip through four states in the southwestern part of the United States. They stopped to have lunch one day at a café just outside a small town in Texas. While they were eating, Ember spotted a sign on the café wall. "Look, Dad," she said, "they have rules in this café."

Dad looked and began to smile. "Do you children recognize those rules?" he asked. Gene looked long and hard at them and finally said, "They kinda sound familiar." Mom smiled and said, "Dad, why don't you read them aloud to us?"

Dad read:

Top Ten Rules of This Café

Rule number one: Just one God.

Rule number two: Honor yer Ma & Pa.

Rule number three: No telling tales or gossipin'.

Rule number four: Git yourself to Sunday meeting.

"I know, I know," Ember said. "Those are the Ten Commandments!"

"Right!" Dad said, "And here are the last six." He read:

Rule number five: Put nothin' before God.

Rule number six: No foolin' around with another fellow's gal.

Rule number seven: No killin'.

Rule number eight: Watch yer mouth.

Rule number nine: Don't take what ain't yers.

Rule number ten: Don't be hankerin' for yer buddy's stuff.

"That's cool," Brett said when Dad finished.

"People across our nation know what makes for a good and decent society," Mom said. "God's commandments are not just for people in Bible times. They're for everybody, all the time."

What matters is to obey God's commandments.
1 Corinthians 7:19 TEV

GOD'S COMMANDMENTS ARE FOR OUR GOOD.

God did not give us the Ten Commandments to take away our fun. No! He gave them to us so we could have the best possible life—now and forever.

Recipe for Joy

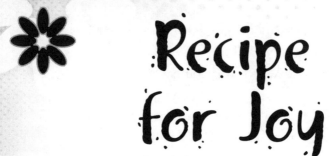

Joy can be real only if people look upon their lives as a service, and have a definite object in life outside themselves and their personal happiness.

"You seem kinda down," Lena's mom said. "Is something the matter?"

"I'm bored," Lena said. "Kammi and Lynda are at camp. I'm tired of reading. School doesn't start for two weeks…"

"Sounds pretty grim," Mom said.

"It is!" Lena replied.

"So, what are you going to do about it?" Mom asked.

"What can I do?" Lena said.

Mom reached for a blank recipe card from her recipe box on the counter. She wrote on it for a minute or two and then handed the card to Lena. "Read it aloud to me," she said.

"Recipe for Joy," Lena read. "Do something nice for somebody you love and praise God while you are doing it."

"This will give me joy?"

"Guaranteed," Mom said. "It works for me all the time. When you look in your heart and do something out of love for another person, you'll feel joy."

Lena looked at the card for a few minutes and then walked to her room. She came back a few minutes later with several music books under her arm. "I'll be back in an hour or so," Lena said as she headed for the back door.

"Where are you going?" her mom asked.

"Mrs. Martinez down the street loves to hear me play the piano, and she's probably more bored than I am. I think I'll go play for her." Her mom couldn't help but notice that Lena had a big smile on her face as she put her music books into her bicycle basket and began to pedal down the driveway.

Be joyful always.
1 Thessalonians 5:16 TEV

TO "BE JOYFUL" IS A COMMAND.

You have the ability to decide if you will have joy. The key to joy is to help others, give to others, or share with others. Everybody has somebody she can help, give to, or share with!

Camp Friendship

No pig ever had truer friends, and [Wilbur]
realized that friendship is one of the most
satisfying things in the world.

It was the first day at Camp Friendship and the new counselors were a little nervous. Just last year Tammy and Kathleen had been campers. Now they were junior counselors! It was awesome. The two friends had met at Camp Friendship five years ago.

"Tammy, would you pray for me?" Kathleen asked. "I'm nervous, and I want to do my best. I want the campers to know how much Jesus loves them."

"Sure, I will. And I want you to pray for me too," Tammy said.

Each girl joined in the prayer, "Jesus, you know we are afraid. But you also know that we want to do our best for you. Help us to show others how much you love them. Amen."

"Let's go!" they said together.

"Hi, my name is Tammy," she told her group of five campers. "It is so great that you are at Camp Friendship. We will do some incredible things like rope climbing, Bible quizzes, and T-shirt painting. The most important thing is for you to know that you are awesome—to us and to Jesus!"

Kathleen told her group about her very first time at Camp Friendship. "I didn't know anyone in the whole camp and I was afraid. I met my very best friend here, and we are still best friends! Camp Friendship is all about how to be a friend and how you can know Jesus as your friend."

Time passed quickly. It was filled with activities, Bible study, recreation, quiet time, and craft time.

"Kathleen, how did it go?" Tammy asked.

"Fabulous! I never thought I could tell someone else about Jesus, but I did!"

"And I never thought I could be a leader. I believe our prayer really made a difference!"

My eyes are always looking to the Lord for help.
Psalm 25:15 ICB

SHARE YOUR JOYS AND FEARS.

Share some good news with a friend. Be willing to listen when someone has a problem that is too big for her. Then go to God for help.

The Visit

Nothing changes a bad situation
like a good word.

"We need to hurry," Mom said to Viona. "We want to make sure we get to see Felix before visiting hours are over."

On the elevator ride to the eighth floor of the hospital, Viona said, "Mom, I'm nervous. What should I say to Felix?"

"Felix has been your friend for years," Mom said. "Just say what you'd say to him if he weren't sick!"

"But he is sick," Viona said. "He has cancer, and that means he might die."

The elevator stopped, and Mom and Viona walked out and stepped into the waiting room. "Vi, nobody but God knows if he is going to die. I'm praying and believing that Felix is going to live, and before we leave tonight, we're going to hold hands with Felix and ask God to heal him. Whether God heals Felix or not is God's job. Our job is to pray with faith."

Mom continued, "Our job is also to encourage Felix. We need to tell him that we love him and that we are looking forward to when he comes home. We need to tell him things that are going on in the neighborhood so he won't feel as if he's missing anything."

"Got it," Viona said. She got up and walked toward Felix's room.

"Hey, Felix," she said cheerfully, "we sure could have used you last night. We got clobbered on the soccer field 8 to 2. Let me tell you about the game."

Felix wanted all the details. For the next half hour, he forgot he was sick.

Give our best wishes to the believers.
Colossians 4:15 TEV

A POSITIVE WORD IS POWERFUL.

The good words you say to another person can change that person's life ... for good! Ask God to show you the very best thing you can say to the next person you meet.

An Example

The first great gift we can bestow on others
is a good example.

Marilyn stood in front of the mirror fixing her hair. "I wish I was pretty," she complained to her mother. "My hair is mouse-colored and my feet are too big. I wish I were taller. When will I ever get these braces off?"

"Marilyn, you are beautiful, and you get prettier every day. You are growing taller, and you've outgrown last year's school clothes. You'll need some new things before school starts."

"I need some shoes, and I'd like some new jeans and tops."

"Let's go shopping on Friday. And I'll make a hair appointment for your back-to-school haircut."

"Thanks, Mom," Marilyn said.

Later that afternoon, Marilyn overheard her little sister in her room talking to her favorite doll, Buffy.

"You know, Buffy," Rebecca started out, "I don't think I'm very pretty. My hair is straight and my teeth are crooked. I wish I had brown eyes like Marilyn. Do you think I'll ever be pretty?"

Marilyn was shocked to hear Rebecca talk that way. Rebecca was so cute and had such a bubbly personality. She brightened any room she walked into. Why would she think that way about herself? It simply wasn't true—any of it!

Then Marilyn realized that Rebecca must have overheard her talking with their mom earlier in the morning. She was repeating what Marilyn had said about herself!

Marilyn went to find her mother. "Mom, I'm sorry about what I said about myself this morning. I want to be beautiful, but just as much, I want my little sister to think she is beautiful."

Remember

Set an example for the believers
in what you say and in how you live.
1 Timothy 4:12 NIRV

PRAISE GOD FOR YOUR LIFE.

Listen to yourself before you complain. Your words and actions have an impact on others. You may be an example for someone who is watching you.

*Every Little Bit Counts

As the purse is emptied,

the heart is filled.

Jennifer stared at the quarter in her hand. *My offering is so little,* she thought, *it won't make any difference if I don't put it into the offering plate at church. Nobody will miss it.*

She stuck the quarter into her pocket, picked up her Bible, and went to Sunday school. The lesson that week was about a widow who went to the temple in Jerusalem and gave an offering—two little copper coins worth about a penny. Jesus had said her giving mattered! Jennifer gulped. *Maybe God heard my thoughts!* Her teacher then told this story:

"There once was a prince in India who dreamed one evening that he owned a beautiful garden. The lake in it was different from any other lake in the world because it was filled with perfume. Its wonderful aroma filled the entire garden and the nearby town. When the prince awoke, he decided to make his dream come true. Although he was very wealthy, he didn't have enough money to fill a lake with perfume. So, he invited every person in the country to come to a party. Each person was asked to bring a small vial of perfume and empty it into the lake.

"People from all over the nation came to the party and, one by one, they each poured their vial into the lake. To everyone's surprise, however, the lake didn't smell any different. The prince finally asked someone to take a sample of water near the spot where the people were emptying their vials. To the prince's dismay, he discovered the water to be just water! He realized that everyone had thought, *My little bit won't matter,* and they had poured water into the lake instead of perfume."

The teacher said, "Nobody thought their little vial of perfume would make a difference. Lots of people feel that way about their offerings. The truth is—every little bit counts."

Jennifer could hardly wait to put her quarter into the plate!

Each one should each give, then,
as he has decided, not with regret or out of a sense of duty;
for God loves the one who gives gladly.
2 Corinthians 9:7 TEV

JOY IS A PART OF GIVING.

Give with joy and God will give back to you so you can receive with joy.

❋ Berry Time

❋

I grumbled as a child with all the
housework and practicing I had to do ...
Now, when I look back, I am grateful
because hard work made me stronger and a
more responsible person.

Kimberly and her brother, Mark, loved being with Grandfather and Grandmother in the country. One of the things they enjoyed most was riding the horses. They loved horses.

It was blackberry season. Every year Grandmother asked for help picking the berries. It was tiring work to get the blackberries that grew on prickly vines.

"If we don't pick them today the berries will rot on the vine," Grandma said. "If we each get a bucket, it won't take long."

Mark and Kimberly loved eating blackberries and enjoyed Grandma's homemade blackberry jam, but they were much less excited about doing the berry picking. They'd rather be riding horses.

They looked at each other. "We'll help, Grandma." They each took a container and set out for the berry patch. It wasn't long before Mark said, "My back hurts. I can't do this much longer."

"Try to fill your bucket, Mark. Then you can be through for today. How's it going, Kimberly?" Grandma asked.

"It's going well, Grandma. I did eat some of the blackberries—that keeps me going longer," Kimberly laughed.

Mark filled his bucket nearly full and declared he was done. He took off to ride the horses. Kimberly kept working. She filled not just one bucket, but two.

Before they went home, Grandpa said, "Kimberly, here's $5 for your two buckets of blackberries. Mark, here's $2.50 for your bucket."

"I didn't know we were getting paid to do this!" Mark replied.

"Your grandmother and I thought you should be rewarded for your hard work. We can't get it all done by ourselves. Thanks so much! And this winter, we can all have blackberry ice cream sundaes."

Hands that don't want to work make you poor.
But hands that work hard bring wealth to you.
Proverbs 10:4 NIRV

YOUR BEST EFFORT IS A REWARD.

You can start and finish a large job by dividing it into smaller jobs and doing them one at a time—until the entire job is complete.

Letting God Work

Patience is one of a few things that you can't learn fast.

The students listened eagerly to Reverend Clem. He was a missionary to the people who lived in a cluster of islands in the South Pacific, and he had very exciting stories to tell about his meetings with them.

"Have very many people accepted Christ?" Baylor asked.

"I don't know of anyone who has accepted Christ yet," the missionary replied, "but I'm not discouraged. I've only been there four years."

He looked out at the group of students and realized that many of them thought four years was a long time and that he had failed as a missionary.

"People need to learn to trust you in that part of the world before they will believe you," Reverend Clem said. "They have to watch your life to see if you really mean what you say."

"But isn't it hard to keep preaching if nobody believes you?" Jerilyn asked.

"Yes," Reverend Clem said, "but I try to remember what other missionaries have experienced. In one church in West Africa the missionary worked for fourteen years before someone accepted Christ. In East Africa, it was ten years. A missionary worked in New Zealand nine years before someone received Jesus as her Savior, and in Tahiti it took sixteen years!"

"Well," said Davie, who was sitting on the front row, "I guess I can keep telling Frank about Jesus! I've only been talking to him about Christ for a year!" All the students laughed because everybody knew that Frank was the school bully.

"The key," said Reverend Clem, "is to talk to Frank about Jesus with love in your heart for Frank, and then live out what you say by doing nice things for him and treating him with respect."

"Missionary work is tough," Davie said. Nobody laughed at that.

Remember

You too must be patient. You must stand firm.
The Lord will soon come back.
James 5:8 NIRV

DON'T GIVE UP HOPE.

Your job is to tell people about Jesus. It's God's job to forgive sins and save souls. Trust God to help you do your job . . . and then trust God to do his job.

✳ Let God Be the Judge ✳

We judge ourselves by what we feel capable of doing, while others judge us by what we have already done.

"You didn't put in money," Vanessa said to her younger sister, Melanie. "I saw you pretend to put money into that envelope but you really didn't."

"So?" said Mel. "I didn't have to give anything. I never told anybody at school I was going to help out on the fund drive to get a new computer. I never promised to give anything."

"Why didn't you just pass on the envelope then?" Vanessa asked. "If it didn't matter to you, why pretend that you were giving when you weren't?"

"Maybe I just wanted to avoid any questions from snoopy sisters," Mel said.

"Maybe you just wanted people to think you're a great girl when you aren't!" Vanessa said as Mel stomped away in anger.

Later, Mel began to think about what Vanessa had said. It was true—she had wanted people to think she gave, especially the teacher who passed around the envelope. Vanessa was right.

What she had done was a form of lying—pretending to do one thing and actually doing something else. She felt awful.

Vanessa also began to think about what she had said. She felt bad and didn't really know why. Finally she decided it really hadn't been her place to confront her younger sister. God saw what Mel had done, and God was able to deal with Mel about it.

"I'm sorry," Vanessa said to Mel before dinner that night.

"I'm sorry too," Mel said.

"I guess we both owe God an apology," Vanessa said. Mel nodded. It was good to have a sister who wanted to do what was right but knew when she had done something wrong. Vanessa also smiled. She felt good that her sister wanted to do what was right, even if she didn't always succeed on the first try.

Remember

"Do not judge others, so that God will not judge you."
Matthew 7:1 TEV

LET GOD DO THE JUDGING.

You Can Do It!

God wants us to judge good and bad behavior and to know what is right and wrong—but we are not to judge people. He'll take care of that.

Weekend Sister

All kids need is a little help, a little hope,
and somebody who believes in them.

Jessica's stepsister spent every other weekend at Jessica's house. Kayla was younger, but they had to share a bedroom. With the new baby and an older brother, there wasn't any other place for her.

For a little kid, Kayla wasn't too bad. But why did she have to come this weekend? It was Jessica's birthday and her friends were coming over. She didn't want Kayla around.

"Jessica, can I come to your birthday party?"

"Kayla, I don't know. My friends are all older than you."

"I promise to be good. You're so pretty and I like all your friends."

Kayla was definitely charming and eager to please her new "big sister." But come to the party? Jessica didn't know what to do. *It must be hard to move from house to house every weekend.* Jessica's father had died several years ago—and that had really been hard to deal with. But Kayla had to share her dad with another family

52

after he and Jessica's mother married. That couldn't be easy either. It wasn't Kayla's fault she was in this situation.

"I have an idea, Kayla. How would you like to be the hostess? That would help both Mom and me a whole lot."

"What does it mean to be a hostess?"

"When my friends come, put their coats in my room. Then show them to the family room where we'll have the party. Help them get a soda, and then we'll start the games. You can keep the music playing on the CD player. When the party is over, you can give each one a party favor before they leave."

"That's a lot to do. But if you help me, I can do it!"

"Thanks, Kayla. You are the perfect one to help."

Here is the command God has given us. Anyone who loves God must also love his brothers and sisters.
1 John 4:21 NIRV

LOVE YOUR BROTHER OR SISTER.

Show your siblings that you care for them. Share something of value with them when they don't expect it.

Music to God's Ears

Praise is music to God's ears.

"I really love music," Shanika said, as she bounced her head to the music from her headset.

"Me too!" shouted Dad, hoping Shanika would be able to hear him.

"What?" said Shanika, taking off the headset.

"Me too," Dad repeated.

"Me three," said Jordie, Shanika's younger brother, as he scurried into the room.

"Do you know where music came from?" their dad asked.

"No," said Shanika.

"Well, there's one old Jewish legend which says that after God created the world, He called in the angels and asked them what they thought of His work. One of the angels said, 'There's something missing—there's no sound of praise to You.' So God made music. It was heard in the whisper of the wind and in the song of the birds. Adam and Eve learned to sing by copying the sound of wind in the trees and the songs of the birds. Then one day they began to wonder if they had music of their own inside their hearts. After all, if every kind of bird had a different type of music, maybe they had a type of music inside them. So they opened their mouths and began to sing."

"Cool," Jordie said.

"And then," Dad said, "the Bible says that way back in the time of Adam and Eve, one of the people was Jubal—he is called the 'ancestor of all musicians who play the harp and the flute.' So musical instruments were invented to go along with songs."

Then Dad gave them a challenge: "On this rainy afternoon when you can't go outside, do you think you two might be creative enough to make up a new instrument out of stuff around the house and use it to go with a new song you might create?"

It took Shanika and Jordie all afternoon to discover that they could!

Sing hymns of praise to the LORD;
play music on the harp to our God.
Psalm 147:7 TEV

GOD LOVES TO HEAR US SING
TO HIM!

You can make up a new song to sing to God. He'd love to hear it!

The Recital

Putting off an easy thing makes it hard, and putting off a hard one makes it impossible.

The page of music sat in front of her like a bad report card—full of things she didn't want to see. Even though the piano bench was getting harder by the second, she knew that silence would reach her mother's ears far quicker than the wrong notes she had played for the last ten minutes.

"I don't hear you," her mother called from the kitchen.

"Okay, Mom, I'm just thinking about the music."

Now her mother was standing in the doorway. "Lindy, your grandma always wanted to play the piano, but her family could never afford one. That's why she's been sending money for your lessons. Just thinking about the music won't help you learn that recital piece. I want you to practice every day this week for at least half an hour before I get home from work. Can I count on you?"

"Uhmm," Lindy mumbled as she turned back to the music. She hoped her mother wouldn't notice she hadn't really promised.

For the rest of the week, Lindy put off her practice. On Friday she didn't actually begin until she heard her mother's car door slam. Lindy wasn't worried—the recital was weeks away.

The day of the recital finally came. Grandma had sent a beautiful dress for her to wear, but Lindy was miserable. Her music piece was not ready! Suddenly they called her name. Her knees shook all the way to the piano. As she sat on the bench, the flash of a camera on the front row caught her attention, and she turned to see the beaming face of her Grandma, who had come all the way from Maine to surprise her for her first recital.

In that moment, Lindy understood that procrastination—putting things off until the last minute—can be another word for embarrassment.

So let us run the race that is before us and never give up.
Hebrews 12:1 ICB

THE HARDEST JOBS BECOME
HARDER WHEN YOU PUT THEM OFF.

Sometimes deadlines seem a long way away ... when they really aren't! Ask God to help you get started on a big project today.

✲ The Rest of the Story ✲

Being judgmental and condemning
is not one of the gifts of the Spirit.

Jeanne had never seen the girl sitting at the desk just inside the classroom door. Students flooded into the room, but no one spoke to her. Just as Jeanne was about to introduce herself, her best friend, Elizabeth, grabbed her arm and dragged her down the aisle.

"Two seats together, Jeanne! Hurry before someone gets them!" said Elizabeth, as she rushed toward two desks side by side. The bell rang, and the principal's voice came over the intercom. "Good morning! Please stand for the Pledge of Allegiance."

The students shuffled to their feet. Since the terrorist attack on the Twin Towers in New York City, the pledge had a new meaning for Jeanne and many other students.

Jeanne noticed that the girl at the front of the room stayed in her seat. She felt anger welling up in her. *How dare a stranger come into our class and show disrespect!* she thought. The pledge ended, and Jeanne whispered to Elizabeth, "Did you see that?"

"What? The new girl? It's a free country." Elizabeth's lack of concern upset Jeanne even more. All morning she kept thinking of things to say to the girl.

When the bell rang for lunch break, Jeanne headed toward the stranger. Just then, Mr. Nichols, the school custodian, came through the door pushing a wheeled object. He stopped in front of the new girl.

"Here ya go, Shanna. No more squeak! I oiled her up good as new for ya," he said as he unfolded a wheelchair with a snap, and the girl slid herself from her desk seat into the wheelchair.

Jeanne stopped in her tracks, ashamed of what she had thought. Then, dragging Elizabeth with her, she went to the new girl and said, "Hi! I'm Jeanne and this is Elizabeth. We're hoping you'll sit with us at lunch."

Help those who are weak. Be patient with every person.
1 Thessalonians 5:14 ICB

DON'T JUDGE UNTIL YOU KNOW THE WHOLE STORY.

Ask God to give you a patient spirit when you see someone doing something you think is disrespectful. Then talk to the person instead of judging her behind her back.

59

Walking Softly

Nothing sets a person so much out of the
Devil's reach as humility.

"Gordon's a wimp," said Jill.

"Why do you say that?" Dad asked. "Because he doesn't play football or talk tough or swagger around as if he's the greatest kid who ever lived?"

"No," Jill said. "He's a wimp because he backs off and never defends himself when other boys tease him. He needs to stand up for himself."

"What do they tease him about?" Dad asked.

"Oh, just stuff," Jill said. "They tease him because he walks away if they're telling dirty jokes. They tease him if he lets somebody break into line ahead of him without telling them to go to the back. Stuff like that."

Maybe I should talk to him, Dad thought. *He's in the scout troop I help to lead. I've never noticed that he backs away from any of the things we do on hikes or overnight campouts. He seems to have plenty of courage, and he always seems to be very helpful to the new scouts in the troop.*

"Gordon," Mr. White said the next time they hiked together. "Guys always seem to call other guys names. What do you do if guys call you names?"

"I don't do anything," Gordon said. "What's the point? I figure if I'm mean to the guys who call me names, it sorta cancels out my being nice to other people. You can't be mean and nice at the same time."

Then he added, "My dad once told me about a president of the United States who said to walk softly and carry a big stick. Dad said he liked the saying, 'Walk softly and believe in a big God.' I like that too."

Gordon's not a wimp, Mr. White thought. *He's just humble. And what a good thing that is! I need to teach Jill the difference.*

Remember

The Spirit produces ... humility.
Galatians 5:22–23 TEV

HUMILITY CAN SPEAK FOR YOU.

Many people say we have to fight our own battles, but God's Word says the Lord will fight for us. Trust God today to do all your "fighting."

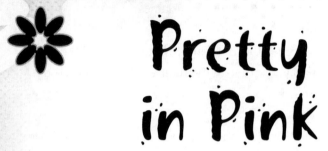

Pretty in Pink

We judge others by their behavior. We judge ourselves by our intentions.

Mara couldn't believe her luck. She'd been in her new school only two days when Lacey, the most popular girl in school, invited her to a "Sungirls" party.

"Who are the Sungirls?" Mara's mom asked.

"Only the most important and popular group in school. They're not really a club, but they're the coolest group at school—all the most popular people. I'm so lucky they liked me right away. Anyone would love to be a Sungirl!" Mara said.

"Well, darlin', don't put all your eggs in one basket," said Mom. "There are a lot of nice people at school you haven't met yet. Don't narrow your circle of friends too much," explained her mother. But thoughts danced in Mara's mind. If she were a Sungirl, she wouldn't need any other friends.

Mara spent all of her birthday money and two months' allowance on the right outfit for the party—a hot pink outfit that looked great.

When Mara went to school Friday morning, she saw Lacey

talking to two other Sungirls and a girl Mara didn't know. The new girl was wearing designer clothes from head to toe.

Lacey said, "Mara, this is Kendra." Lacey hesitated, "Uh, Mara, you can't come to my party tonight after all. Kendra's coming and my mom says I can have only twelve guests. Sorry."

Mara was so stunned that she couldn't move as Lacey marched away with Kendra. When she finally turned to go to class, a girl she'd barely noticed gave her a smile.

"You might not have as much in common with Sungirls as you think." she said, "because you're a nice person. Why don't I introduce you to some other nice people?"

"Thanks," Mara replied, thinking *It would be great to meet someone who would see me for who I am, instead of my trying to be who someone else wants me to be.*

Remember

God, you do what is right. You know our thoughts and feelings.
Stop those wicked actions done by evil people.
And help those who do what is right.
Psalm 7:9 ICB

YOU ARE THE COMPANY YOU KEEP.

You Can Do It!

The way others treat you shouldn't affect your opinion of yourself—just the friends you choose!

Grateful Grace

It's nice to be important, but it's more important to be nice.

"Mom, this is so lame!" Catherine whined. "Why can't I just call Aunt Catherine and tell her I liked the necklace she sent for my birthday? It's sooo much easier and quicker. Besides, it would probably cost less than putting a stamp on this ol' envelope!"

Her mom was not amused. "Catherine, you were named for your Aunt Catherine and you are very special to her. She went to a lot of trouble picking out and sending something she thought you would like. You should be willing to take a few minutes to write a short note of thanks."

Catherine gave up. There was no use arguing with her mother when she used that tone of voice. She used the note card that her mother gave her and wrote four short sentences telling her aunt that she liked the necklace and planned to wear it on Sunday. She also made sure to say thank-you.

When her aunt came to visit two months later, Catherine made sure her Sunday outfit included the necklace. Sitting together in the pew, Aunt Catherine leaned forward slightly so as to get a better view of her pretty niece wearing the necklace. As she did, her Bible slipped from her lap and several envelopes tucked inside slipped out and onto the floor. Helping her aunt pick up the papers, Catherine saw her own handwriting on one of the envelopes.

"You kept my note!" Catherine said to her aunt.

"Of course! Your note made me feel so good. I love to read it whenever I'm a little down and missing my family here. Good manners always make people feel better. It's always good to be thankful—to God and to other people."

I wrote the letter so that you could see, before God, the great care that you have for us. That is why we were comforted.
2 Corinthians 7:12–13 ICB

GOOD MANNERS SHOW OTHERS THE
LOVE OF CHRIST.

If you will do little things to make others feel more comfortable, acceptable, or appreciated—you will feel more comfortable, acceptable, and appreciated too!

The Gift

Being grown up is something you decide
inside yourself.

Taylor hated being the youngest in the family. She felt she could never do anything as well as her older siblings, Tripp and Tracey. There weren't a lot of years between them, but enough that she always felt like the "little kid." *That's my place in life forever and ever,* she thought.

It was almost Christmas, and Tripp and Tracey were hinting what they might give about Taylor. If she guessed right, it was awesome—they were going to let her go skiing with them and their friends when they went to Gram and Gramp's condo in Colorado. She could hardly believe it! She had gone skiing with the whole family, but not with Tripp and Tracey and their friends.

Taylor was excited and filled with anticipation. She took an inventory of her ski equipment. Everything was repaired and in good shape.

The week before Christmas Tripp and Tracey said they needed to talk to her. "Taylor," they began, "we've been thinking. You might be too young to go with our friends—maybe next year would be better."

Taylor was crushed, but she didn't argue. It was their trip and their friends. On Christmas morning there was a wrapped box from Tracey and Tripp with Taylor's name on it. This was no doubt the consolation prize. Even so, she opened it eagerly. Inside was an envelope with her name on it. She took out the card. It was an invitation from Tripp and Tracey ... an invitation to go on the ski trip!

"Wow!" Taylor said. "Thanks! I thought you'd changed your minds."

"Well, we decided to give you a test to see if you were mature enough to go. And you passed with flying colors!"

The child [Jesus] grew and became strong. He was
very wise. He was blessed by God's grace.
Luke 2:40 NIRV

GROW UP ON THE INSIDE.

Sometimes saying nothing at all is the wisest choice!

# Finders Keepers

A bad conscience has a very good memory.

Barbara couldn't believe her luck! Aunt Leslie had sent her a box of fabulous clothes that cousin Pam had outgrown. There were dresses, pants, tops, and a beautiful party dress.

Barbara's mom left her alone with her treasure. "Pop out and let me see each outfit as you try it on!"

Barbara was zipping up a pair of hip-huggers when she noticed a bulge in the pocket. Her eyes grew wide when she pulled a one-hundred-dollar bill out of the pocket. She knew cousin Pam's family was better off than her own, but how could she forget a hundred dollars?

But maybe she didn't forget it, Barbara thought. *Maybe Aunt Leslie put the money there as a special gift for me. After all, I could use some new shoes to go with the party dress. No one knows I found the money—no one, that is, except God.*

"Barbara! What's the holdup?" called her mom.

Barbara opened the door slowly and walked to her mom. "Mom, look what I found in the pocket of these pants."

"My goodness!" Mom said. "I'm sure that's been missed! I'll call Aunt Leslie and find out what's going on."

"Oh, thank heavens!" Aunt Leslie said. "Pam was going to have to babysit for weeks and weeks to earn that back. It's money from the school fundraiser. Pam was supposed to take it to the bank to get change for one of the booths, but somehow she 'lost' it on the way. She'll be so happy you found it."

Back in her room, Barbara thought, *What if I'd bought shoes instead of giving back the money? I would have been miserable once I found out where the money came from. Whew! Thank You, God!*

God, examine me and know my heart.
Test me and know my thoughts.
Psalm 139:23 ICB

CONSCIENCE IS A GIFT FROM GOD.

Don't give it a second thought—just do the right thing the first time.

*The Mountain Trail

All of God's giants have been weak men who did great things for God because they believed that God would be with them.

"Don't look down," the group leader said.

Easy for you to say, Ruth thought. She had wondered for the past hour why she had signed up for this hike, but now she really questioned her own decision.

Ruth enjoyed nearly all the activities and events at camp. She loved to swim, to play volleyball, and to paddle the canoes on the lake. And she liked hiking in the woods. But she did not like high places!

And there she stood, at the end of a hike that took them up a high mountain trail that had become very narrow.

In her mind, Ruth knew that the trail was safe and that there was plenty of room to walk between the side of the mountain and what seemed like a drop-off to her left. But in the pit of her stomach, she felt sick with fear. Then, she remembered the Bible verse they had talked about that morning during a quiet time in the cabin: "He is my God and I am trusting him" (See Psalm 91:2

TLB). Ruth began to say over and over, "I'm trusting You, God, I'm trusting You." Step by step she repeated these words ... until finally she stood at a wide place in the trail and could see they were headed downhill and back to camp.

At the end of the week, sitting by a big bonfire, the camp leader asked every camper to think of the hardest thing they had accomplished at camp. "Hiking the mountain trail," Ruth said.

Then the leader asked, "And what's the best thing you did this week?"

Ruth was surprised to hear herself say, "Trust God to help me hike the mountain trail."

Don't fail me, Lord, for I am trusting you.
Psalm 25:2 TLB

WHEN WE TRUST THE LORD, WE TRIUMPH!

The best thing we can do when we face a difficult thing is to trust God. Ask the Lord to help you trust him more.

71

Every Day

It is better to be faithful than famous.

"Well, how was it this year?" Dad asked Brock and Fran that evening after they both had had time to unpack and take hot baths. Brock and Fran had been at youth camp for a week, and when Dad picked them up at the church, they had seemed happy and tan, but also hungry and tired. He figured time for a talk would come after supper and before bedtime.

"It was great," Fran cried. "I really liked the speaker this year. We had some good talks in our discussion groups too. Swimming in the pond and riding the inner tubes down the canal—those things are always fun."

"What did you like best?" Dad asked Brock.

"I really liked the guys in my cabin this year. And we had a really neat counselor. His name was Luke and he was a real Christian."

Dad said. "I'm a little curious to know why you called him a real Christian."

"Well," Brock said, "he made us spend time after lunch out in the woods with our Bibles, just reading whatever we wanted to read. He called it a 'quiet time.' And after the lights were out at night, he led us all in the Lord's Prayer."

"Those are very good Christian things to do," Dad agreed. "I would hope your counselor at a Christian camp would do those things."

"But Dad," Brock said, "we didn't just do those things once or twice. We did them every day."

"There's a lot to be said for faithfulness," Dad said. "It really is what makes us real Christians to those who don't know Jesus as their Savior."

Remember

The Spirit produces ... faithfulness.
Galatians 5:22 TEV

BEING FAITHFUL MEANS
FOLLOWING THE LORD.

You Can Do It!

Get in the habit of doing things God's way. The best habits become your best character traits.

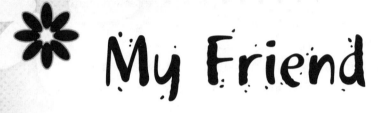

My Friend

My best friend is the one who brings out the best in me.

"I don't know why you always sit with Gloria at lunch," Rhonda said to Laurel. "You could sit with us sometime. It might make you a little more popular."

"Gloria and I have been friends since we were born," Laurel laughed. "I like having lunch with her."

"But why?" Rhonda asked. "Gloria says some really stupid things sometimes."

"Really?" Laurel said, "I hadn't noticed. I know Gloria never thinks what I say is stupid."

"She doesn't know how to dress—just look at the outfit she put together today."

"I think her outfit is fun," Laurel said to Rhonda. "Gloria always thinks I look great."

"Gloria isn't really good at anything—not in class or in sports or anything," Rhonda said.

"But Gloria is always quick to applaud those who do well and quick to say 'congratulations' to the winners," Laurel said. Then she added, "And you know what, Rhonda? Gloria would never criticize you or anybody else the way you are criticizing her. That makes her special to me."

"Well, I guess you and Gloria are two of a kind. Both losers," Rhonda said with a very mean tone of voice.

Laurel grinned. "Gloria and I may be losers in your eyes, and even in the eyes of lots of kids, but I know this—she's my friend and I'm her friend. And because of that, we both see ourselves as winners!"

Friends always show their love.
Proverbs 17:17 TEV

STAND BY YOUR FRIENDS.

Build up—encourage, applaud, and love—your friends! Don't let others put them down without speaking up.

Keep at It!

By perseverance the snail reached the ark.

"This book report is taking forever to write," Jenna complained.

"Really?" Dad asked. "How long have you been working at it?"

"Almost an hour!" Jenna said. "The report isn't due until Friday, but I thought I'd get it written tonight so I wouldn't have to worry about it. Now I'm not sure I'm going to finish by Friday."

Dad smiled and said, "Jen, aren't you doing a book report on *The Old Man and the Sea* by Ernest Hemingway?"

"Right," Jenna said. "It's taking me longer to write this report than it took to read the book!"

"But," Dad said, "do you know that Hemingway is said to have gone over the manuscript of *The Old Man and the Sea* eighty times before he sent it to a publisher?"

"Eighty times?" Jenna said. "No way."

"Way," Dad said. "Lots of writers worked very hard at what they wrote. When I was in London last year, I saw an exhibit about a famous poem. There were seventy-five drafts of the poem on display!"

"Really?" Jen said.

"Really," Dad replied. "I once heard that it took Noah Webster thirty-six years to write his first dictionary. And there's a famous commentary I use when I study the Bible—it took the author forty years to write it."

Then Dad added, "Stick with it, Jen. Maybe you won't get the whole report written tonight, but remember, God didn't make the world in a day—it took a whole week."

Let us not become tired of doing good; for if we do not give up, the time will come when we will reap the harvest.
Galatians 6:9 TEV

EVERYTHING OF QUALITY TAKES TIME.

Even if your steps are small or your progress is slow, keep moving forward and soon you'll reach your goal.

Campaign Strategy

Let all you tell be truth.

Darla didn't like what she was hearing from her "campaign committee"—her three friends Kent, Mindy, and H.R.

"She's spreading lies about you, Dar," Kent said.

"Like what?" Darla said.

"Like saying you copy your English papers off the Internet," said Kent.

"And ... you and your family are part of a radical group that keeps a big stash of guns in your basement," added H.R.

"I like the rumor about you and Matt making out in the school parking lot during a football game," Mindy laughed.

"People who know me know these things aren't true!" Darla exclaimed.

"That's the point," said Kent. "Not ALL the kids know you, and those who don't know you don't know that what Priscilla is saying about you isn't true. We've got to fight fire with fire."

"What do you think I should do?" asked Darla.

"We could start telling people that Priscilla is bulimic,"

Mindy suggested. "She is really thin."

"Great!" Kent said. "And we could say she's probably moving next year so she won't be around to be a student body officer anymore. Her dad does work for a company where lots of people are being laid off.

"No," Darla said. "I'm not going to fight fire with fire. I'm going to fight fire with water—the truth. I'm going to ask her during the debate if she had anything to do with the lies being told about me and see what she says. Even if she says she had nothing to do with the lies, I'm going to say, 'I'm so glad to hear that because you know these things about me aren't true. One of the most important things about being school treasurer is being honest.' I'm not going to lie to win. I'm going to tell the truth and win!"

Whoever wants to enjoy life and wishes to see good times, must keep from speaking evil and stop telling lies.
1 Peter 3:10 TEV

THE TRUTH ALWAYS COMES OUT.

No matter what lies people may tell about you, God knows the truth, and in his timing he will cause other people to know the truth too.

Even Better

You can do what you have to do,
and sometimes you can do it even better
than you think you can.

Nicole thought the "homework" assignment was just about the dumbest idea she'd ever heard of. Her mother had enrolled her in something called a "homemaker's course" in summer school—she said it was a course she took when she was Nicole's age.

At first, Nicole had liked the class. She learned to bake bread and set a table for a dinner party. Now they were sewing. And of all things, the teacher assigned them to make an apron!

"Nobody uses aprons anymore," Nicole said to her mother, as she pinned the pattern pieces onto the fabric she had chosen.

"Well, you might use this one," Mother said. "And even if you don't, there are all kinds of things you can learn by making an apron."

Nicole found she liked using the sewing machine.

"I have an idea," Mother said when she was just about finished. "Let's see if we can make this an even better apron. God always wants us to do our best, not just what's okay."

"How?" Nicole asked. "We're all using the same pattern, and there were only three types of fabric to choose from."

Mother handed her a small hand towel. "Let's make three buttonholes in the top of this towel and then put three buttons on the waistband of your apron."

"Great idea!" Nicole said. "That way I don't have to reach for a towel—it will always be there."

When she was finished, Nicole said to her Mother, "You know, I just might use this apron after all."

Remember

No matter what you do, work at it with all your might.
Ecclesiastes 9:10 NIRV

ALWAYS DO YOUR BEST.

Look for ways to do a little extra, go a little further, or give a little more. The "little" you add to your effort can be the difference between just okay and excellent.

The Exchange

Compared to friendship, gold is dirt.

Dawn couldn't believe Mr. Johnson put her with Ginger. She hardly knew Ginger, except that Ginger was quiet, didn't dress very well, and had too many freckles to be cute. To top it all off, this particular experiment was—yucky was the first word that came to mind. They had to handle a frog! Then, they were to draw the frog with as much detail as possible and to describe how it felt to hold the frog. The teacher said something about under-standing more about God's creation, but all Dawn could think of was how she would make it to the next hour.

To Dawn's surprise, Ginger reached into the glass container where their frog was sitting and picked it up. "I live on a farm," she said to Dawn, "and I have two brothers. They used to dare me to touch frogs all the time."

Dawn said. "Looks like they lost the dare."

"Actually," said Ginger, "I beat them a couple of times in a frog-jumping contest." Ginger went on to tell Dawn about how the contest worked—it sounded like fun. Finally Dawn got up her nerve to hold the frog, and she was grateful when Ginger said, "Great job!"

When it came to drawing, Dawn discovered that Ginger was an artist. When Ginger said, "Writing really isn't my thing," Dawn quickly jumped in, "But it's my thing." During the next hour, the two girls talked and laughed almost nonstop. And when the hour was up, the teacher said their drawing and description was one of the best in the class! "You can be my lab partner any time," Dawn said.

Ginger smiled and replied, "I'd like that."

People learn from one another, just as iron sharpens iron.
Proverbs 27:17 TEV

YOU CAN LEARN SOMETHING FROM EVERYONE.

Never underestimate the possibility of a person becoming your friend. Plant a seed of friendship and see what God might grow!

The Marker

Waste no more time arguing about what a
good man should be. Be one.

The Thompsons were traveling to the home of relatives for a
big family reunion over the Thanksgiving holiday when they
stopped to get a breath of fresh air, some bottled water out of the
ice chest in the trunk, and "stretch their legs," as Dad said.

The rest stop was next to a small old-fashioned cemetery.

"Look at the tombstones," Rosemarie said. "They are really
big and they have carvings and designs on them."

"Look at that one," Norm said. "It's got a big angel on top of it."

"It looks as if it might be in a children's area of the cemetery,"
Mom said.

"How can you tell?" Norm asked.

"The graves are very close together," Mom said.

"Can we go see?" Rosemarie asked.

"Sure," said Mom. "I'll walk with you while Dad rearranges
some things in the back of the car."

The children discovered that the gravestone with the angel
was, indeed, the grave marker of a young girl who had died when

she was only six years old. Norm read aloud the name of the girl and the dates of her life on the white marble base. Then Rosemarie read aloud this tribute carved into the stone:

"A child of whom her playmates said, 'It was easier to be good when she was with us.'"

There really wasn't anything more to be said. Mom and Rosemarie held hands as they walked back to the car. Even Norm was quiet.

"She may have been just a little girl," Mom said, "but she really made her life count. She had an influence on people for good."

"I know she's influenced me," said Rosemarie.

Norm added a quiet, "Me too."

The Spirit produces ... goodness.
Galatians 5:22 TEV

PEOPLE REMEMBER THE GOOD YOU DO.

If you want other people to feel good about you, think good thoughts toward you, say good things about you, and do good to you ... be good!

Tennis Class

Courage is being scared to death—and
saddling up anyway.

"Hurry a little," Mom said to Donita. "Don't forget to bring your racket."

Donita didn't feel like hurrying. She didn't feel like going to the tennis courts at all.

"You're acting as if you aren't excited about the first day of tennis lessons," Mom said. "You loved tennis class last year."

"That was last year," Donita said.

"So what's so different about this year?" Mom asked.

"This year the boys and girls are together for doubles."

"Right," Mom said. "But I would think that would make it even more fun. You were one of the best players last year in both singles and doubles. It will be fun to learn to play doubles with the guys."

"I'm not sure," Donita said. "They hit the ball pretty hard."

"Three things," Mom said. "One, I think you're going to find that you are better than some of the boys. Two, you know how to get in the right position to hit the ball and that's the main thing in doubles tennis. It isn't how hard you hit the ball as much as where and when you hit it."

Donita hadn't thought about that, but it sounded right. In fact, she seemed to remember her tennis teacher saying the same things last year. "What's number three?" she asked.

"Number three is that Jesus is going to help you do this if you ask him. Learning to play tennis is a good thing. Jesus always helps us learn to do good things when we trust him to help us."

"We'd better hurry," Donita said. "I want some extra time to warm up."

Be brave, be strong.
1 Corinthians 16:13 TEV

JESUS NEVER STOPS HELPING US.

You never know how good you can be until you try. Be brave and try hard.

Stay on Track

Criticism is easy; achievement is more difficult.

"I'm so sick of Raylynn's criticism," Kara said. "She's always telling me that I'm dumb. Now some of the other kids have started saying the things she's saying. I don't think I can take it anymore. I'm about to tell her off."

"What are they criticizing you about?" Mom said.

"They call me Miss Goody-Two-Shoes and tell me that I'm stupid for going to church or believing in God. They make fun of me for praying before I eat lunch and for walking away when they tell dirty jokes."

Mom listened patiently and then said, "Can I tell you a little story that might help?"

"Sure," Kara said.

Mom said, "I once heard about a famous violinist. A music critic who wrote for a New York City newspaper was very hard on this man. As a result, when he played in other cities, some of the critics in those cities were also very critical of him. Critics tend to copy critics, you know."

"What happened to him?" Kara asked.

"The editor of the New York City newspaper offered the violinist space in the paper to reply to the critics. The violinist said, 'They can write against me. I will just keep playing. My music and the fact that the people come to my concerts are my best defense.'"

Mom continued, "I think, Kara, that if you stay silent and just keep doing what you are doing, the criticism will eventually stop. Doing something good is always a more powerful act than saying something critical."

Remember

Moses said . . . "When you complain against us, you are really complaining against the LORD."
Exodus 16:8 TEV

GOD'S OPINION IS THE ONE THAT COUNTS.

It is easy to criticize another person. It is hard to do what's right, to compliment others and to be kind to your critics. Refuse to take the easy way out!

Green Pickle Greeting Cards

For those who are willing to make an effort, great miracles and wonderful treasures are in store.

Gym class just wasn't her thing. Brooke was always the last one chosen to be on a team. She didn't care a thing about hitting a ball or shooting a basket. It made no sense to her. She didn't even care about winning or losing. It didn't matter—they were just games.

Brooke simply had no interest in sports! Art was her favorite class. That was where she had talent and lots of it! She knew if there was such a thing as an art team she would be picked first, not last!

She thought, *Well, why not?* Just because it hadn't been done before didn't mean it couldn't be done. Brooke had an idea … and maybe, just maybe, it could work.

Brooke's idea was to make and sell greeting cards. Her art class could provide the art. Each kid could make the cards however they wanted—computer art, water color, scrapbook art, oil painting, or even button art. The possibilities were endless.

Hartley, Brooke's friend, was great in English and creative writing. She asked him to join the team, "Hartley, I've got this idea. It just has to work. I know it will!" And she explained the plan. "We need some awesome greetings. You would be great at that. Do you have someone who could help you?"

Hartley was on board immediately. "I have a friend who would be great at organizing a group to make envelopes." Then they would also need a sales team. They put their heads together and came up with a plan that included everyone!

"Let's call the project the Green Pickle Greeting Cards," said Hartley.

"Why that?" asked Brooke.

"When life hands you a green pickle, it's time to make relish!" Hartley said.

Remember

God chose you to be his people.
1 Peter 2:9 NIRV

INCLUDE OTHERS IN YOUR PLAN!

Do you know someone who feels left out? Invite her in!

Getting Help

He who asks may be a fool for five minutes,
but he who does not ask remains
a fool forever.

Tina loved to read, but she hated math class. Numbers and equations were boring to her, and she especially didn't like problems that had Xs and Ys in them!

"I'll never understand this," Tina said one night while she was doing her homework. "It's just too hard. And what good is it anyway?"

"What are you working on?" Dad asked.

"My math homework. I've got a whole sheet of it, and I just can't do it," Tina said, throwing down her pencil.

"Let me see," Dad said. "I'm like you, honey. I like reading more than math, but let's see if there's anything I can help you with."

Dad stared at the sheet of Xs and Ys and equal signs and said, "We need help. Do you know the first thing you need to do when you don't understand something?"

"No, what?" Tina asked.

"You need to ask for help from somebody who knows," Dad said. "And do you know the second thing to do?"

"No," said Tina.

"The second thing," Dad said, "is to keep asking until you find somebody who knows and who can explain it in a way that you can understand. That works not only for math but for lots of things in life."

"So who do we know?" Tina said.

Dad reached for the phone. "I'm going to call Jerry. He's a real math expert at my company. I'm going to see if we can pay him a visit!"

"And what if Jerry can't help?" Tina said.

Dad grinned and replied, "Then I'm going to call Darren … and if he can't help, I'm going to call John.…"

Remember

Getting wisdom is the most important thing you can do.
Whatever else you get, get insight.
Proverbs 4:7 TEV

GOD KNOWS EVERY ANSWER.

You Can Do It!

If you don't know the answer to a question or the solution to a problem, keep asking until you get the best answer. That's how great discoveries are made.

Boldly Beautiful

I commend my soul into the hands
of God, my Creator, hoping and assuredly
believing, through the only merits of Jesus
Christ, my Savior, to be made partaker of
life everlasting.

Charlene was watching the Miss America Pageant with her mother. "All of the women are so beautiful and so talented. I think any one of them would be a great Miss America," she said.

Mom replied, "Yes, but beautiful on the outside is even better if the woman is also beautiful on the inside."

"But how can you tell if a woman is beautiful on the inside?" Charlene asked.

Mom said, "You can't always ... at least not at first. I remember, though, one Miss America contest when I was just about your age. There was a beautiful young woman from Arizona named Vonda Kay Van Dyke. She made it into the finals and in those days, the last five girls were asked a question by the emcee, a man named Bert Parks. Mr. Parks asked her, 'Do you carry a Bible as a good luck charm?' People apparently had found out that Vonda

Kay had a Bible and that she often carried it with her. People had also found out that she was a Sunday school teacher. Vonda Kay said to Mr. Parks—and to all of us watching on television across America—'It's not a charm; it's the most important book I own.' And then she added, 'I wouldn't classify my relationship to Jesus Christ as a religion, but rather as faith. I trust in Him completely."

"Wow!" said Charlene. "That was pretty bold. Did she win?"

"She did!" Mom said, "She was Miss America for 1965."

I am not ashamed of this Good News about Christ. It is God's powerful method of bringing all who believe it to heaven.
Romans 1:16 TLB

YOU KNOW JESUS—NOW TELL OTHERS.

You never know when the words you speak might prompt a person to accept Jesus as his or her Savior. Be bold to tell people about Christ.

A Kind Garden

The greatest pleasure in life is to do a good turn in secret and have it discovered by accident.

"What are you drawing, Tracy?" Lexie asked. Five-year-old Tracy seemed very intent on her coloring. She had dozens of crayons scattered around a fairly large piece of paper.

"I'm drawing my favorite poem," Tracy said. Lexie smiled—she liked the way her little sister Tracy said poem—it sounded more like "pome."

"Which poem is that?" Lexie asked, thinking Tracy would probably tell her a nursery rhyme.

"It's the one Auntie Sharon reads about the garden," Tracy said. She stopped her coloring to hand Lexie a book of children's poems. Then she opened the book and pointed to a particular poem that had a drawing of a garden. The gate to the garden was in the shape of a giant heart.

"Read it to me," Tracy said.

"Sure," said Lexie, and she began to read aloud this little poem by Longfellow:

Kind hearts are the gardens,
Kind thoughts are the roots.
Kind words are the flowers,
Kind deeds are the fruits.
Take care of your garden,
And keep out the weeds;
Fill it up with sunshine,
Kind words and kind deeds.

"That's a great poem, Tracy. I can see why you like it," Lexie said. And then Lexie looked closer at the artwork Tracy was creating. She had placed a heart at the center of each flower she had drawn.

"That's really great," Lexie said. "If kind words are the flowers, your words all have love in them."

"Right!" said Tracy. "And I'm making this picture for you."

The fruit of the Spirit is ... kindness.
Galatians 5:22 NKJV

KINDNESS IS DOING GOOD ALWAYS.

One of the best habits you can develop is the habit of kindness—thinking kind thoughts, speaking kind words, and doing kind deeds. Practice kindness today!

The Sweetest of Birthdays

One kind act will teach more love of God
than a thousand sermons.

Shelly carefully poured sugar into the measuring cup and added it to the mixing bowl. As her older sister, Ellen, watched, she mixed the sugar, butter, and grated lemon peel; put in flour, salt, and baking powder; and finished by adding milk and lemon juice.

"This cake is going to be so good!" Shelly giggled. Usually, her mom helped her, but today Mom had decided that Shelly was ready to go "solo"—to bake a cake all by herself with just Ellen watching.

When the cake came out of the oven, it was perfect! Shelly let it cool before adding some lemon icing. She put several candles on top and followed Ellen to the house five doors down where Mrs. Carson lived.

"Happy Birthday!" Shelly and Ellen chimed when the elderly lady opened her front door.

Mrs. Carson was amazed at the sight of the two girls holding a birthday cake.

"It's lemon—your favorite!" Shelly said as she and Ellen followed Mrs. Carson to the kitchen.

Ellen lit the candles and the two sisters sang "Happy Birthday." As the three of them ate slices of cake and drank tall glasses of milk, Mrs. Carson said, "I can't believe you remembered my birthday—and my favorite cake! When my husband died three months ago, I didn't think I would want to celebrate my birthday this year; but, the two of you have made me realize that there's plenty of reason to celebrate another year of life."

"I'm glad you feel that way," Shelly said, taking another bite of cake. "Now that Mom is letting me bake, I've lots more recipes I want to try."

"Maybe we could do some baking together," Mrs. Carson said. "It sure is nice to have company."

There are three things that remain—faith, hope,
and love—and the greatest of these is love.
1 Corinthians 13:13 TLB

LOVE YOUR NEIGHBOR.

Look around your neighborhood. Is there someone who's lonely, who would appreciate a visit? Take time to spend time with other people.

Different Gifts

Remember your possibilities. Forget your limitations.

The sounds coming from the violin sounded as if the poor instrument were screaming for help. Even Rosa's violin teacher looked a little bit shocked at all the squeaks and creaks that Rosa was producing.

Music, it wasn't.

"That's enough for today," Miss Temple said brightly. "Be sure to practice."

Rosa was glum at dinner. She sat on her bed crying when her dad knocked softly on her door.

"Rosa?" he said, opening the door a crack. "May I come in?"

"Y-yes," Rosa sobbed. Soon Dad was sitting beside her with his arm around her shoulders.

"I c-can't do this!" Rosa wailed. "I hate the violin! I've been taking lessons for almost two years, and I'm still no good."

"Maybe it's not your talent," Dad said.

"W-what do you mean?" Rosa hiccuped.

"God gives all of us different talents. Some of us can sing really well, or write, or play baseball, or give speeches—but not all of us excel at everything."

"I can sing," Rosa said. "The choir director at church asked me if I'd like to sing a solo sometime."

"There you go," Dad said.

"But I still want to play an instrument," Rosa said. "My friend Jasmine taught me some chords on the piano, and I did pretty well."

"Sometimes," Dad said, "we can get better at something if we just keep working at it. But sometimes, all the practice in the world won't help."

"Like me and the violin," Rosa grinned.

"I think so," said Dad. "I think it's time to move on."

God has also given each of us different gifts to use.
Romans 12:6 CEV

FIND OUT WHAT YOU DO BEST.

Don't be discouraged if there's something you can't do as well as one of your friends. You can be sure that God has given you the ability to do something else extremely well!

*The Highest Honor

It is the enlarging of the human adventure
that sports are all about.

It wasn't long before basketball season would begin. If Abigail wasn't practicing at school, she was shooting baskets at home.

Margie and Abigail were best buddies. Abigail was short, but she loved the game. Margie was the high scorer and played every game. Both Margie and Abigail made the team.

Abigail didn't get to play in many games, and her parents were concerned that she would want to quit. "I love being part of the team. They're the greatest!" Abigail said to her parents.

When she did get to play, she often threw the ball to other players so they could shoot for the basket. Her dad asked her why she didn't take the shots.

"Dad, there are other girls who don't get to play much either, but they can make baskets better than I can. I love basketball, but I don't always have to be the one taking the shots."

The Jaguars had a winning season. When the time came for awards at the school assembly, all the parents went, including Abigail's. They didn't expect her to win anything, but they knew she wanted them to be there to support the team.

The awards for High Scorer, Best Improved, and Most Valuable Player were all passed out. Abigail cheered for each of her teammates who won a trophy,

Then Coach Hubbard said there was one more award—the Sportsmanship Award. It was new this year, but the teachers voted to award it. And the first Sportsmanship Award was given to Abigail Griffin!

Abigail couldn't believe her ears. Her classmates cheered her on. "Abigail! Abigail! Abigail!" They kept it up until she got to the awards table. And then they let loose with a standing ovation.

Abigail thought to herself, *This really is the greatest team in the world!*

Remember

Iron can sharpen iron. In the same way,
people can help each other.
Proverbs 27:17 ICB

A GREAT ATTITUDE WINS EVERY TIME.

If you don't get a lot of playing time, or even if you didn't make the team, you can cheer for them. Every team needs fans to help them win.

✻You Are Not Invited ✻

Out of every disappointment
there is treasure.

"It's going to be the greatest party ever!" Claire exclaimed. "Todd's mom has hired a band, there will be three kinds of cake, and fireworks, and everything! I can't wait!"

Nina sighed. It did sound great. Todd's mom was the best when it came to planning parties.

It was several days before Nina realized that most of her classmates had received invitations to Todd's party … but she hadn't. At dinner, Nina picked at her food and felt sick.

"What's wrong?" her mom asked.

"Todd's having a party tomorrow, and I wasn't invited," she whispered.

"Is Todd a good friend of yours?" Nina's dad asked.

"No, I don't really know him that well. He's in some of my classes, and he says 'hi' sometimes, but that's all."

"But you feel left out," Mom said. "That's normal. I know it hurts to be left out; but believe me, it's a lot more fun to be with people who really want to be with you."

"And who really like you!" Dad said, smiling.

"Like us!" Mom exclaimed, jumping up to hug her daughter. "Tomorrow night, I think we'll have a party of our own—just the three of us."

"Can we have cake?" Nina asked.

"Of course," Mom said.

"Three kinds?" asked Nina, with a twinkle in her eye.

"Now you're pushing it!" Mom laughed. "But we'll fire up the CD player and do some singing and dancing."

"Please don't let Dad sing," Nina giggled. "We want this party to be fun!"

Many who are first will be last, and the last will be first.
Matthew 19:30 NRSV

BE GLAD FOR THOSE WHO
LOVE YOU.

Here on earth, you may not always be at the top of the invitation list for everyone's party, and that's okay. When you accept Jesus Christ as your personal Savior, you have the best invitation you'll ever receive!

❋ Be Sure to Share ❋

The measure of our success will be the measure of our ability to help others.

———— ❋ ————

The subway car was packed with people when Vera and her big brother, Monroe, got on. They had to stand as the train made several stops to pick up and drop off passengers.

Finally, there were two empty seats right next to Vera and Monroe. Just as Vera was about to plop down, she heard Monroe say, "Here are two seats; come sit down."

Vera looked up to see a pregnant woman and an elderly man. Monroe was helping them to the seats.

"Thank you so much," the woman said, sighing with relief as she sat down. "I thought I would have to stand for the next seven stops."

"Thank you, young man," the elderly gentleman said. "If your parents were here, I'd tell them what a fine job they have done in raising you."

Monroe smiled.

"I'm just doing what my dad always does," he said. "He and Mom taught me that we all need to help each other out."

Vera was proud of her brother's generous heart.

The next time there's an empty seat and somebody else needs it more than I do, I'm going to be just like Monroe ... and Dad, she thought. I'm going to smile and say, "Here's a seat for you!" And maybe there are other things I can do to be nice to people, like helping our neighbors carry in groceries.

The subway car swerved a bit. Monroe put his hand on her shoulder and gave it a squeeze. "Hang on, Sis," he said. "It won't be long now. We're almost home."

When we have the opportunity to help anyone,
we should do it.
Galatians 6:10 NCV

MAKE ROOM FOR OTHERS.

Jesus Christ is the best example we have of generosity. He gave up everything—his very life—for us. There are lots of things we can do to help other people every day.

Appearances Are Only That!

Thenceforth, in the nature of things, [the wolf cub] would possess an abiding distrust of appearances. He would have to learn the reality of a thing before he could put his faith in it.

Collyn and Shelby were in the same class. Collyn really admired Shelby—she got straight As all the time. She could read without missing any words. And her math papers were always perfect. Besides that, she was pretty!

Collyn wished she was as smart as Shelby—then life would be perfect. Collyn wasn't all that great as a student. She hated reading out loud or having to speak in front of the class.

It was a rainy day at the end of the semester, and Collyn and Shelby stood inside waiting for the bus to come. They had their report cards, and Shelby looked scared. Collyn couldn't imagine what could be wrong.

"Shelby, are you all right? You don't look like you feel very good," Collyn said.

"Uh, I'll be all right … I think," she replied.

"I'm not so sure," Collyn continued.

"Well, it's my grades. I made a C in geography," Shelby

finally admitted.

"Wow, you always get As. I made a C and I have a hard time remembering how to spell the names of all those countries. But you're so smart. I thought As just came naturally to you," she said.

"I wish!" Shelby said. "My dad doesn't let me do anything until all my homework is done. I have to study ahead into the next assignment. I have been studying but he's going to be upset because I think I need a tutor and I don't know if we can afford one."

"Shelby, I'm sorry. I just thought ..."

"It's okay. Everybody thinks my grades come easy. I guess that's because I try not to complain. I was just disappointed in my grade. See ya later," she called as she stepped onto her bus.

I guess everything isn't always the same on the inside as you see it from the outside, Collyn thought.

Give thanks to the Lord, because he is good.
His faithful love continues forever.
Psalm 107:1 NIRV

THINGS AREN'T ALWAYS WHAT THEY SEEM.

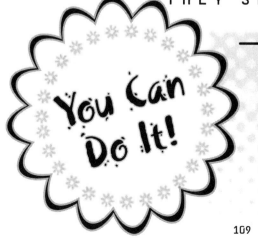

Give thanks to the Lord for what and who he made you to be. He made you exactly according to his perfect plan.

❋ Permanent Words ❋

Anger itself does more harm than the condition which aroused anger.

Janelle couldn't believe she'd had to give up her beautiful bedroom when her mom's Aunt Ida came to live with them. Now her little sister bugged her while she studied, and she couldn't help shouting at her. Her little sister shouted back.

Aunt Ida flung open the door and clapped her hands. "Girls, girls! Be quiet!"

Janelle's anger rose and her voice rose even more. "Well, then go where it's more peaceful. This is our house and we'll yell if we want to. Besides, if I had my own room, we wouldn't be yelling at all!"

Stunned, Aunt Ida turned and walked out of the room, closing the door behind her. The door opened only seconds later and Janelle's mother entered.

"Janelle," her mother said, "I have told you for a long time that anger hurts everybody—including the one who is angry. Now you know why. You don't know that when Aunt Ida's husband died last month, he left her without any money and lots of bills to pay. She had nowhere else to go. Now both you and she must live with the angry words you spoke."

"But I didn't really mean to say it!" Janelle began to cry. "I didn't mean to hurt her."

"But you did and you can't take it back. The words we speak—true or not—can't be undone."

"I'll apologize," Janelle said.

"Yes, I think that's a good idea. But you're also going to have to show her that this is her home too. Most of all, you need to talk to God about controlling your temper."

Later that evening, Janelle knocked on Aunt Ida's door. "I came to apologize," she said, "and … bring you some flowers for your room."

A person who quickly gets angry causes trouble. But a person who controls his temper stops a quarrel.
Proverbs 15:18 ICB

ANGRY WORDS HURT EVERYBODY.

When someone makes you angry, count to ten before you speak.

The Car Wreck

When you have accomplished your daily task, go to sleep in peace. God is awake.

Bridget and her friend Mary Grace were sitting in the back-seat of Mary Grace's mother's car, talking about things that had happened at school that day.

"It was so funny when Bart spilled that paint on his canvas in art class and Mrs. Johnson said it looked like a great work of art!" said Bridget, remembering how everyone had laughed.

"Yeah," Mary Grace said, giggling, "and it was even funnier when Bart agreed! He said ..."

CRASH! The conversation was cut short when the car smashed into another car that had run a red light at the intersection.

"Are you kids okay?" Mary Grace's mom asked anxiously, turning to look into the backseat.

Bridget and Mary Grace were pretty shaken up, but they weren't hurt.

"Don't worry," her mom said. "Everything will be all right."

The police came, drivers exchanged insurance information, and Mary Grace's mom drove Bridget home. Her parents were upset about the accident but grateful that their daughter was not hurt.

"I had my seat belt on," Bridget said. "You told me to always wear it. And it was funny, but I kind of felt peaceful the whole time."

"What do you mean?" her mom asked.

"Remember how you say that God is always watching over us," Bridget explained. "I felt like He was right there in the car. It was a neat feeling."

Bridget's dad smiled and hugged his daughter tightly. "It's a relief to know that when Mom and I can't be with you, God is on the job."

"He sure is," Bridget said. "He's the greatest."

He is always watching, never sleeping.
Psalm 121:4 TLB

RELAX. GOD'S EYES ARE OPEN.

No matter how hard we try to be careful, accidents can still happen. It is such a relief to know that God is always with us, and always knows what is happening. We don't have to worry.

The Scarf

Our prejudices are our robbers, they rob us
of valuable things in life.

Shiva and her best friend, Ashanti, were shopping with their moms, who were also best friends. All four "girls" made this shopping trip to a large city two hours away from home every year just before school so that Shiva and Ashanti could start the year in style!

It was a blistering hot day as they climbed into the car to leave the mall. Suddenly Shiva cried, "Look!" and pointed to a woman crossing the steamy pavement in a full head scarf and what looked like a long black coat that went all the way to the ground. "How stupid is that on a hot day like this?" she asked.

"Oh," said Ashanti, "That's one of those people who blew up the buildings in New York City. That's a disguise for bombs! Those people are scary."

Ashanti's and Shiva's mothers looked at each other in disbelief and shock, and then turned to their daughters in the backseat.

Shiva's mom said, "Shiva! Ashanti! That girl might have been born and raised in Iowa! Her dress doesn't tell us anything except that she may be part of a religious group that hasn't accepted our Savior. And being afraid of her and saying things that prob-ably aren't true won't help her see Jesus in you!"

The girls glanced sideways at one another.

Then Ashanti's mom continued, "Ashanti, as an African American, you should know as well as anyone how unfair preju-dice is!"

"You're right, Mom," said Ashanti as Shiva nodded in agree-ment. "Bad and good people come in all colors and dress."

"I guess just now Ashanti and I were behaving like bad peo-ple, huh?" added Shiva.

Remember

Don't say or think bad things.
Ecclesiastes 10:20 ICB

PREJUDICES REVEAL THE HEART.

Don't decide what you think about a person until you've gotten to know her ... and hope she'll do the same for you!

The Extra Towel

The person that loses her conscience has nothing left worth keeping.

"Marta, where did this towel come from?"

Marta looked up from unpacking her backpack. The family had just returned home from a two-week vacation, and it felt good to be putting all her stuff back where it belonged. Mom was helping her unload the suitcase she and her little brother had shared. "Oh, the hotel at the beach," Marta said.

"You took a towel from the hotel?" Mom asked.

"I wanted a souvenir," Marta said.

"Souvenirs are one thing," Mom said, "but a towel is something else! It's not a souvenir."

"But we take the little shampoo bottles and soaps," Marta said.

"Yes," Mom said. "Those things are intended by the hotel owners for us to use and take. But not towels!"

"What's the difference?" Marta asked.

"Soap and shampoo are called 'consumables,'" Mom said.

"Consumables?"

"Right," Mom said. "Consumables are things that are used

up—like food and pop. You wouldn't leave half a sandwich or half a bottle of pop lying around for the next person who came into the hotel room, and you also don't leave a used bar of soap or half a bottle of shampoo for the next person in the hotel room. But a towel is something that can be washed and reused by another person. It's not for us to take! It's like the sheets or the bedspreads."

"Well, what do I do?" Marta said. "I didn't mean to steal it. I thought it was okay to take it."

"We're going to send it back with a little note saying we're sorry," Mom said. Marta knew that "we" in this case meant "Marta."

"I'd better start writing," she said.

Remember

"You might see your enemy's ox or donkey wandering away. Then you must return it to him."
Exodus 23:4 ICB

WHEN IN DOUBT, LEAVE IT OUT.

If you find something you have taken by mistake that doesn't belong to you, do your best to find the owner. If you don't know for sure what to do, ask a parent or teacher to help you figure it out.

Sick with Jealousy

Jealousy is a blister on the heels of friendship.

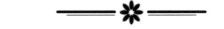

"Have you seen that new spy movie?" Josie asked Bailey.

"No, not yet," Bailey said.

"I have," Josie said. "My dad took my brothers and me to see it on Saturday. Then we went out for pizza."

"Sounds like fun," Bailey said, wishing she'd been invited.

"Guess where we're going this weekend?" Josie asked.

"Where?"

"To that new amusement park with all the rides and water slides and that scary roller coaster! I can't wait to ride that!"

"Yeah," Bailey said.

As the girls parked and locked their bikes on the rack, Bailey noticed that Josie wasn't on her usual bike. "Like my new bike?" Josie asked, noticing Bailey staring at it. "It was an early birthday present. Dad said it was a reward for getting an A in history."

Bailey was miserable all day, thinking about Josie. At dinner that night, she complained about the food. "Why can't we have pizza?" she whined.

"Bailey!" her mom said. "Fried chicken is your favorite."

"Nuh-uh," Bailey said. "Pizza is."

"What's going on?" her dad asked.

"Josie-gets-to-go-to-movies-and-eat-pizza-and-go-to-amuse-ment-parks-and-get-a-new-bike!" Bailey said in a rush of words.

"Are you jealous of Josie?" Mom asked.

"Maybe a little," Bailey admitted.

"Does it feel good to be jealous?" Dad asked.

"No."

"Did you know that the Bible says jealousy is like poison?" Mom asked.

"It sure feels that way," Bailey said.

"Then let's pray right now and ask God to help you get rid of it," Dad said. "That way, you can enjoy this great fried chicken."

I say it is better to be content with what little you have.
Otherwise, you will always be struggling for more.
Ecclesiastes 4:6 NCV

BE GLAD FOR WHAT YOU HAVE.

Some people have lots of things. Ask yourself these questions: Do I have love? A family that takes care of me? Enough to eat and enough to wear? Good friends? Then you've got the really important "stuff."

The Ballerina

*It doesn't take strength to hold a grudge;
it takes strength to let go of one.*

Suni loved to dance more than anything. She had been a featured ballerina in recitals, and she had played a mouse in the city ballet's production of *The Nutcracker Suite* for two years. Everyone said next year she might dance as the main character. But the rules said she would first have to be accepted into the ballet company's special dance school, and she was too young by several months. Still, the teacher agreed that if no one in the class objected, Suni would be allowed to study with the older dancers.

"Ladies, Suni can't be an automatic part of our dance class until after it's too late to try out for *Nutcracker*. But if all of you vote to accept her, she can be a member of our class. Raise your hand if you want her to join us."

The girls knew Suni was talented, and hands shot up like rockets—all but one. At the end of the ballet barre stood a curly-headed girl who didn't raise her hand.

"Put your hand up!" several girls said to her.

"No way! There's barely enough space for all of us in this class. Besides, who needs the competition?"

Suni thought her heart would break. She'd have to wait a whole year to audition for a lead role.

She was still feeling down the next day in science class when the teacher pulled her aside. "Suni," she said, "I'm assigning you a new lab partner. I know you'll help her—at least I hope so. You're her last chance. If she doesn't pass science, she's going to be held back another year. She's at your lab table now."

Suni turned to find the curly-headed ballerina sitting at her table.

"Help me, God," Suni prayed. She had never prayed a more sincere prayer.

If your enemy is hungry, feed him. If he is thirsty, give him a
drink. Doing this will be like pouring burning coals on his head.
And the Lord will reward you.
Proverbs 25:21–22 ICB

SHOW KINDNESS TO ALL.

Try to make peace with someone you feel has done something wrong to you—and maybe even do something especially nice for that person.

*A Dangerous Weapon

If you think you know it all,
you haven't been listening.

When Mrs. Westerman asked a question about the Civil War, Luanne eagerly waved her hand.

"Robert E. Lee!" she exclaimed.

"That's right," said the teacher. "He was the leader of the Army of Northern Virginia."

"Eventually, he was named commander of all the South's armies," Luanne added, looking around at her classmates to make sure they'd noticed how smart she was.

"Boy, she's a smart aleck," mumbled Kari to Ginny. "I can't stand her."

"She is smart," Ginny said.

"But she doesn't have to rub it in," Kari whispered.

After class, Luanne went marching up to Kari. "Do you need any help with your homework?" she asked sweetly. "I noticed that you couldn't answer that question about Abraham Lincoln."

"No, I don't need your help," Kari retorted. "I'd rather flunk."

"And you probably will," smiled Luanne, walking away.

"Is there a problem?" asked Mrs. Westerman, noticing the scowl on Kari's face.

"Not now that Miss Know-It-All is gone," Kari said.

"It sounds like Luanne really taught you something today," said the teacher.

"Her? No way!" Kari protested.

"Can you tell Kari what you learned, Ginny?"

Ginny thought for a minute. Finally she said, "That it's great to be smart, because you get good grades, but you shouldn't brag about it all the time?"

"That's it," said Mrs. Westerman. "You should follow Luanne's good example, which is to study hard and do your best. Just don't use your brains as a weapon to make other people feel as if they're not as good as you."

Let us not become proud. Let us not make each other angry.
Let us not want what belongs to others.
Galatians 5:26 NIRV

DON'T BRAG ON YOURSELF.

If God has given you a really good brain, use it to do his work. But don't get the idea that being smart means you're better than other people. It's a gift God gave you—be grateful.

The Good Deed

The secret pleasure of a generous act is the great mind's great bribe.

Kathy didn't complain at all when her mom asked if she would run the lawn mower over their tiny yard since her brother was away at camp. She loved helping!

With her mother's help and instruction, she began pushing the little lawn mower back and forth across their lawn. It was harder than she thought it would be, but she enjoyed the summer sun.

Kathy wasn't the least bit tired when she finished the grass in their front yard, and she wasn't ready to go back inside. Just then she noticed that the neighbors' lawn had grown while they were away for a few days. So Kathy began mowing it.

She began to tire before she was done, but she didn't want to leave the job unfinished. Besides, maybe they'd be so grateful they'd offer to pay her! Then she'd have plenty of cash for that new swimsuit she wanted.

"That was nice," her Mom said when she went in. "I know the Smiths will appreciate it." Kathy wondered how much.

Several days later, Kathy picked a quiet moment to ask, "Mom, why didn't the Smiths say thank you for what I did? They sometimes pay somebody else to mow for them."

"Is that why you did it—for the money?" Mom asked.

"Well, not at first ..." Kathy's voice trailed off.

"Sweetie, when you do something for someone without expecting anything back—even a thank you—you get the biggest reward of all."

Just then the phone rang and Kathy picked it up. "Kathy, this is Linda Smith. Jim and I just realized that somebody mowed the grass for us. We suspect that you or your brother did it. We want to thank you and tell you that if you want the job, you're hired!"

Remember

"The Lord bless you. You have shown kindness."
2 Samuel 2:5 ICB

SHARING IS PLANTING A SEED.

Surprise someone with a kind act every day. It's a way of sharing God's love.

Hidden Talents

God doesn't give people talents that he
doesn't want people to use.

Aunt Susan was headed upstairs to find her camera when she found her niece sitting all alone on the stairs.

"What's up, Fallon? Why aren't you in the living room celebrating with the rest of the family?"

"I don't think I belong to this family," said Fallon.

"And why not?" asked her aunt.

"Because I can't do anything. Michael is in a band, Mom and you are artists, and now we're throwing this big party for Patti to celebrate her winning first place in the Junior Miss contest. It's not fair that I'm not good at anything!"

"Why you certainly are so! Your talent doesn't hang on a wall and can't be recorded or photographed. But you're the only person in our whole family with your special talent."

Fallon looked puzzled.

"Fallon, I don't know anyone more organized than you are. You just know how to get everyone going in the same direction so whatever we do together comes out great and is so much fun. Like this party, for instance—you organized that and made sure the house was ready for guests when we got back from the contest. And the family schedule you made and put on the fridge is the only way your brother and sister ever know when to go to their lessons and who's going to pick them up. Now top that all off with your great memory for numbers and names, and—well, in lots of ways, you make the rest of our talents possible because you help us where we are weak."

Fallon had never thought of organization as a talent, but Aunt Susan was right. If there was an organization contest, she'd win it hands down. She decided to go to the party—after all, it might need a little organizing!

Remember

We all have different gifts.
Romans 12:6 ICB

THERE ARE MANY DIFFERENT
KINDS OF TALENTS.

You Can Do It!

Practice the talents you have
and appreciate the talents of
those around you.

The Apology

A sincere apology heals the heart.

Mikaila and Ned and two of their friends were at the playground, which was right across the street from Mikaila and Ned's house. They had been playing freeze tag and decided to sit and relax for a minute before starting a game of kickball.

Pam, one of the group's classmates, walked by with a friend.

"Let's ask them to play kickball," Ned suggested.

"No," said Mikaila. "Pam's no good at kickball. She's not really any good at sports."

"Maybe her friend is," said Jim.

"She doesn't look very athletic," Rachel decided.

"And she has the wrong shoes on," said Otto.

"Yeah, and did you see what she was wearing?" Mikaila chimed in, giggling. "I don't want somebody who dresses like that on my team!"

What the friends didn't realize was that Pam and her friend were now standing just a few feet behind them. They had heard every word. Pam's friend started to cry.

"You are really rotten!" Pam shouted at them when they

turned around to see who was crying. She then put her arm around her friend's shoulders and led her away.

"Boy, I feel really rotten," Ned sighed.

"You didn't say anything mean like we did," Otto said.

"No, but I didn't try to stop you, either," Ned replied.

"It's my fault," Mikaila said. "I started it."

"We're all guilty," said Rachel. "My mom would be really mad at me if she knew."

"We can still do the right thing," said Ned. "Let's go apologize and ask them to play with us."

"What if they say no?" asked Rachel.

"We have to at least try to make up with them," Jim said.

"Ned's right," said Mikaila. "Let's go tell them we're not as rotten as we acted just now."

This is what the Lord of heaven's armies, the God of Israel, says: Change your lives and do what is right!
Jeremiah 7:3 NCV

WHAT YOU SAY IS WHAT YOU GET!

It's not nice to criticize someone. Imagine how you would feel if someone did that to you. Speaking good things about others brings positive words back to you.

☀Reality Check

[For the national Miss Teen USA Pageant] I wanted to get an inexpensive dress to prove the point that it's not the dress, it's what's inside the dress.

"That's a cute sweater, Courtney. It looks really great on you. Where'd you get it?"

"My father gave it to me. He bought it in Chicago when he was there on business," Courtney said.

"It goes great with your hair."

"Thanks, Anya. See you later."

"Courtney," Sandi said in a whisper as Anya walked away, "Isn't that the sweater your mother got you from the resale shop?"

"Well, yes. But I don't want Anya to know that. She has designer labels on all her clothes."

"But it doesn't really matter, does it?" Sandi said. "It's a cute sweater. Who cares what store it came from or what the label says on the inside? Nobody sees the label anyway."

"Let's go, Sandi," Courtney said. "We'll be late for gym class." She knew Sandi was right, but she didn't want to admit it. Quietly she prayed, "Lord, help me to tell the truth. I know it's my heart you want others to see."

In the locker room after class, Courtney overheard a girl say to Anya, "You have the greatest clothes, Anya, and all the latest labels. You must have a huge clothes budget."

"I really don't," Anya said. "I have a cousin in Kansas City who is just a year older than me. Her parents own a clothing store and she gets new clothes every year. She sends me what doesn't fit her anymore—and it's always still in style."

"Wow, you're really lucky."

"Well, it works out for everyone. I don't think it's a good idea to spend a lot of money on clothes, especially just for designer labels. They're not worth it."

"You're right. Clothes don't make the person—it's what's on the inside that matters most."

[Jesus said,] "And why do you worry about clothes? Look at the flowers in the field. See how they grow. They don't work or make clothes for themselves."
Matthew 6:28 ICB

THE OUTFIT DOES NOT MAKE THE PERSON.

Base your opinion of others on who they are, not what they wear.

Sharing Your Faith

"Once you become a Christian," the Sunday school teacher said, "it's very important to tell other people. The Bible tells us to share the 'good news' with others."

Evan and Celia, who had been Christians for several months, told their family and most of their friends that they had asked Jesus to come into their hearts. There were two friends, though, who weren't interested: Jerry and his sister Ruby.

"We don't want to talk about religion stuff," Jerry had said. "Let's go play horseshoes."

Evan and Celia did not mention God to Jerry or Ruby anymore. They felt sad, though, because they really liked Jerry and Ruby and wanted to make sure that they would all be in heaven together someday.

Evan decided to be brave and invite their two friends to the Sunday school picnic.

"No way—no church stuff," said Jerry.

"There'll be horseshoes," Celia said.

"Horseshoes?" Jerry perked up. "Well … maybe we could go."

The four friends went together and enjoyed all the great food and games. At the end of the day, Ruby said, "I didn't think I would like 'church people,' but they're not so bad."

"Yeah, nobody tried to force me to get saved," Jerry laughed.

"We don't do that," Celia said. "We just tell you the truth about God and let you make up your own mind."

"I guess I can handle that," Jerry said. "Maybe I'll come check out that church of yours sometime."

"You do that," Evan said. "We like to share the things we love with our friends."

Those who lead many others to do what is
right will be like the stars for ever and ever.
Daniel 12:3 NIRV

SPEAK UP ABOUT JESUS.

Sometimes it's hard to talk about Jesus with people who don't want to hear about him. But those are the very people who need to hear about him, so don't give up.

Do the Math

Arithmetic is where numbers fly like
pigeons in and out of your head.

Abigail did well in her candy sales for the school fundraiser. She sold them to the people who worked at her dad's office and to her neighbors and grandparents. The sales part was fun—she was good at selling. But keeping track of the money ... who bought what, who paid, and who still owed ... those were not her strong points.

When the sales were over, Abigail turned in the orders at school. Three weeks later her parents helped her pick up the candy, pay for it, and sort out the orders. This did not go well! There seemed to be a very big problem.

"Dad, I can't figure this out. I turned in $156 to the school. The total order was for $245. The difference is $89. But my records show my customers owe me only $47. That means I am $42 short. Can you check my math?"

"Your math looks fine, honey. But you're right—you're $42 short," Abigail's father said after checking over the numbers. "There's only one thing to do, Abigail. You'll need to come up with the money and pay it to the school."

Abigail didn't have that much money. It would take forever to come up with it. She thought to herself, *I could say I turned in all the money and blame the shortage on someone else. Or I could ask my clients to contribute extra to the fundraiser. I could even charge a delivery fee when I drop off the orders. I could* ... Finally she decided none of those were good options.

"I guess it's up to me to come up with the extra money." She emptied the coins from her bank and borrowed some money from her savings account.

"That's a hard lesson, Abigail," her parents said. "But you made the right decision."

May my honest and good life keep me safe.
I have put my hope in you.
Psalm 25:21 NIRV

HONESTY WILL NEVER DISAPPOINT YOU.

When you make a mistake, admit it. Then go on and make it right with those you wronged.

A Clean House

If each one sweeps in front of his own door,
the whole street is clean.

"Time for spring cleaning!"

When Doug and Elaine heard their mom say those words, they wanted to run and hide. Now that they were older, Mom expected them to help with more of the top-to-bottom house-cleaning that she liked to do twice a year.

"I don't see why we have to empty out these closets," Doug grumbled as he pulled snow boots, hockey sticks, and a pair of pink mittens from a back corner.

"Wait! Those are the mittens I lost!" Elaine exclaimed.

"Lucky you," Doug mumbled, using a dust mop to clean the closet floor.

"These windows don't even look dirty," Elaine said as she sprayed on some cleaner and gave them a brisk rubdown with paper towels. She was surprised to see dirt on the towels when she finished.

"How's it going in here?" Mom asked, coming to inspect the room.

"Our house isn't that dirty," Doug said. "You clean it all the time. Why do we have to do this?"

"Remember how we didn't clean the garage for a really long time?" Mom asked.

"Yeah, it took three days to do it, and there were spiders! Ugh!" Elaine said.

"And that box of books was ruined because we didn't know that it had been sitting in a puddle of water," Mom said. "When you keep up with the cleaning, it's easier to do it, and it takes less time. As soon as you finish up in here, we'll be done. We can go out for pizza."

"I'm on it!" Doug exclaimed, grabbing some furniture polish. "This dust is a goner."

When a man won't work, the roof falls down.
When his hands aren't busy, the house leaks.
Ecclesiastes 10:18 NIRV

CLEANER IS BETTER — REALLY!

You might not think that housework is any fun, but you have to admit that it's great when everything is clean and you can find your things. It's important to keep the clutter out of your heart too.

Never Alone

It is your concern when your
neighbors' wall is on fire.

Ginny was a bright student and had great girlfriends. She and her family were new to the city but they had settled in quickly.

In spite of her good work, Ginny's teachers were a little concerned for her. Ginny's clothes sometimes needed to be washed. Her dad showed up at the parent-teacher conferences, so there didn't seem to be a home problem ... or was there? Even though she lived close to school, Ginny never had her friends over to visit her.

One day Ginny missed an important rehearsal for the school play. That just wasn't like her—she had a lead part.

Walking home after school, Kara and Colleen thought they would stop to see if Ginny was all right. They knocked at the door, but no one answered. The drapes were pulled shut. They heard the television, so they rang the doorbell. Soon Ginny came to the door.

"My mother's sick today so I stayed home," she told the girls.

"Is there anything we can do?" they asked.

Ginny looked as though she might cry, "My daddy said my mother drinks too much. That's why I can't have anyone come to my house. Please don't tell anyone."

Kara and Colleen knew they needed to help. "Can we tell Miss Georgia, our school counselor? She can help you."

"I went to talk to her when my parents got divorced. I was really, really afraid. But Miss Georgia was wonderful—she helped me through it," Kara said.

"I didn't know you had problems. I thought I was the only one," Ginny said. "Do you really think she can help?"

"I'll go with you to see Miss Georgia," said Colleen. "You don't have to be afraid."

"I'm glad you care about me," said Ginny. "I'll see you in school tomorrow."

I am poor and needy, but you, the Lord God, care about me.
Psalm 70:5 CEV

ASK FOR HELP WHEN YOU NEED IT.

Are you struggling with a problem that is bigger than you are? Ask someone you trust for help.

Planning Ahead

Good enough never is.

Twins Benjamin and Brittany lived on a farm and raised animals to show at county fairs.

One day, the twins' dad decided to give them a job they hadn't done on their own before. "Kids, I want you to mow the big alfalfa field, bale it, and get the hay into the barn before the first snow. You can work on it at your own pace, but just be sure it's done before it snows. Otherwise your animals won't have anything to eat this winter."

The twins figured the first snow should be at least a month away.

The first week, they got most of the mowing done. They missed a corner here and there. *That shouldn't amount to much hay,* they thought. Week two they finished mowing and began baling the alfalfa. The job took longer than either Benjamin or Brittany thought it would, so they decided to run the baler a little faster over the field. They began to miss a lot of hay, and the wire holding the hay into bales was loose.

Then school and activities began to cut their work time short and two weeks later, when the first snow was on its way, there were still bales in the field. Dad and Uncle Charlie had to help them get it stowed in the loft of the barn.

When they finished at midnight, Dad said, "Kids, I'm afraid your 'almost good enough' job wasn't good enough. I don't think you have as much hay as you are going to need. You'd better start thinking about how you're going to earn enough money to buy hay when that runs out this winter."

That was not what Benjamin and Brittany wanted to hear … but they knew Dad was right.

The ants are not a strong people,
but they prepare their food in the summer.
Proverbs 30:25 NASB

A JOB WORTH DOING IS WORTH
DOING RIGHT.

Go a little slower with that job that you would rather not do; get it right the first time so you don't have to do it over again!

More to Celebrate!

Whoever is happy will make others happy too.

Elena's mother drove her to school on the first day of the school year. Elena was excited about her new school in the United States. The family had moved from Puerto Rico just two months before.

The family settled in with the help of church people and found a home for themselves. Elena's father found a job teaching Spanish at a junior college.

During winter break, Elena and her parents planned to go back to Puerto Rico to visit her grandmother and grandfather for Christmas. Elena wanted to visit her grandparents, but she didn't want to leave her friends and miss all the Christmas parties in their new city.

Elena's mother had an idea. In Puerto Rico, the people also celebrate Three Kings Day on January 6. She promised Elena that when the Gonzalez' returned home, they would celebrate that holiday with Elena's new friends.

Elena invited her friends to spend the night with her on January 5 when the celebration begins. On the night before Three Kings Day, Elena and each of her friends put grass and water under their beds, like the children do in Puerto Rico. This was a little unusual, the girls thought, but they did as Elena told them and soon fell asleep.

When they awoke the next morning each girl was surprised to find a gift under her bed. Elena explained the custom: The camels drink the water and eat the grass, and the kings leave a gift for each child who helps the camels.

The girls were all delighted with their surprises. "It's like having two Christmases," one of the girls said.

When others are happy, be happy with them.
Romans 12:15 CEV

NEW FRIENDS MEAN NEW ADVENTURES!

Invite someone from another country or culture to share traditions with you and your friends.

The Test

Nothing is really lost by a life of sacrifice;
everything is lost by failure to
obey God's call.

This was the children's first trip into the desert to watch their dad test the horses. Five unsaddled stallions snorted and stamped as they waited. The horses could smell the water at the oasis only a little way beyond their stopping place, and they were very, very thirsty.

Leah and Logan had watched her father train the horses for months. He was able to whistle in a certain way that the horses recognized as a command to come to him. This small group of Arabian stallions did what none of the other horses in the corral had ever done. When Dad whistled, these five instantly came and stood directly in front of him.

So why had Dad refused to give them food or water for the past two days? And why had he brought them all the way to the desert for water at the oasis?

Suddenly, Dad gave the signal to release the stallions. Desperately thirsty, they bolted for the oasis. But just as they reached the pool, Dad whistled!

Two of the horses plunged their noses into the water to take a long drink. Two others took a short drink and then turned to run back to Dad. But the fifth horse stopped the instant he heard the whistle and, in spite of its tremendous thirst, the horse turned and ran back until he was standing in front of the children and their father.

"This is the horse, kids! Of the five, this is the only one that we can depend on to obey its master no matter how strongly it wants to disobey. You can trust this horse with your life. The others will never be trustworthy."

Then her father looked deep into their eyes. "Leah and Logan, when it comes to obedience, people are not so different."

[Jesus said] "If you love me, obey me."
John 14:15 TLB

GOD COMMANDS US TO BE OBEDIENT.

Next time your parents ask you to do something you'd rather not do, just say "Yes!" instead of "Why?"

Keeping Promises

Avoid the last-minute rush—do it yesterday.

Saundra's room was a mess. The bed wasn't made. Books were everywhere but on the shelves. Toys, games, and dolls covered nearly every inch of the floor. Clothes and shoes appeared to have forgotten that they belonged in the closet; they were thrown on chairs and even under the bed.

What a mess!

It was Saturday morning and Saundra had agreed to go to a friend's house to watch videos and have lunch. Later, her friend's mom would take them to the pool. Saundra's dream was to become an Olympic swimmer someday, and she needed all the practice she could get.

"Where do you think you're going?" Saundra's mom asked as she saw her daughter heading for the front door.

"To Micki's house," she said. "I told her I'd come over."

"Have you cleaned your room?" Mom asked.

Saundra rolled her eyes and sighed. "I'll do it later, Mom, okay?"

At that moment, Cloudy, the cocker spaniel, came bounding into the room and jumped up on Saundra.

"Do you remember our agreement?" Mom asked. "You begged your dad and me for a dog, and you agreed to keep your room clean if we'd let you have one."

Saundra looked into the eyes of the adorable puppy.

"I think he needs a walk too," Mom said.

Saundra was silent for a moment as she thought about her promise.

"I'll call Micki and tell her I'll be a little late," she finally said. "I'll clean my room as soon as Cloudy and I get back from our walk. Okay, Mom?"

"Okay," her mom smiled. Saundra was growing up.

Remember

Those who have been given a trust must prove
that they are faithful.
I Corinthians 4:2 NIRV

DO WHAT YOU SAY YOU WILL DO.

God always keeps his promises. As his children, we should be like him in every way. That means we should keep our promises too.

Jarrett's Joy Cart

Generosity lies less in giving much than in
giving at the right moment.

Jarrett Mynear was only two years old when his family found out he had cancer. By the time he was ten, he was an expert on living in a hospital. Jarrett had lots of treatments that made him feel very bad. He also had several operations, one of them to remove part of his leg.

Jarrett had every reason to be sad. But he wasn't. One day it occurred to Jarrett that he wasn't the only kid in the children's hospital who was sick. He realized there were lots of other kids feeling as bad as he did. He decided that someone should do something to make them all feel better—and that someone was Jarrett!

He came up with a plan to fill a pushcart with stuffed animals and other toys. Kids could choose a toy to keep from the cart. With the help of his mother, Jarrett raised donations of money and toys from people and businesses in his hometown. Jarrett spent all the spare time he had setting up and running "Jarrett's Joy Cart" for the kids in the local children's hospital.

The first day Jarrett took the Joy Cart around to the hospital rooms, several local radio and television stations covered the event and even more donations rolled in because of the news reports. Even when Jarrett was feeling very sick, rolling the cart around the hospital and seeing the happiness it brought to other kids helped him feel better.

Today, Jarrett's Joy Cart is giving out free toys to hospitalized children in several cities. Jarrett's family hopes others will start joy carts of their own all across the United States.

"Live [within my] love ... I have told you this so that
you will be filled with my joy."
John 15:10–11 TLB

FEEL BETTER BY HELPING OTHERS.

Know someone who needs a little help or just cheering up? Think of something that you can do just for her that will help brighten her day. Small things count!

Doing What's Right*

Friends, if we be honest with ourselves,
we shall be honest with each other.

When Katie saw the necklace, she knew she had to have it. It would go perfectly with the blouse that her mom had just bought for her. One look in her wallet, though, told her that she couldn't afford it.

"Just take it!" whispered her friend Tisha. "It's not that expensive. It won't hurt the store if you take one little necklace."

Katie thought about it and remembered what her mom had said about shoplifting—how it was a crime, and how it made the stores raise their prices. And she remembered a sermon her pastor had preached on "doing what's right, not what feels good." She decided that she just couldn't do it.

"Stealing is wrong," she said. "My mom says it doesn't matter if you take a pack of gum or a car. Taking something that doesn't belong to you is stealing. That's the way God sees it anyway."

"But the necklace is perfect for you!" Tisha insisted. "You should have it!"

"It's okay," Katie said. "It wouldn't feel good to wear it if I had to do something wrong to get it. Anyway, my birthday is next month. Maybe if I tell my mom that I like it, she'll get it for me."

"I guess you're right," Tisha said, as she saw a security guard walk by. "I guess it's not worth getting into trouble."

"No, it's not," Katie said. "And it's not just about avoiding trouble. It's about doing the right thing."

"Sounds good to me," Tisha said. "Let's just go get some ice cream—my treat!"

Be very careful, then, how you live—not as unwise
but as wise.
Ephesians 5:15 NIV

THINK BEFORE YOU DO SOMETHING.

When the Bible says that something is wrong, like stealing, it's wrong! Don't let friends talk you into doing something that you know is wrong.

✾What's Most Important? ✾

"Jenna, how are you coming on your pledges?" Jenna's dad asked at breakfast.

"Great! So far I've got $22 for every lap I run. I'm going for my all-time best! I think I can raise more before the deadline."

The annual fundraiser was for a local school for disabled children. The school was important to the Carlisles since Jenna's younger sister, Julie, was a student there. She had multiple disabilities, and the family depended on the school in many ways for her education and physical therapy.

This year, Jenna had asked her Sunday school class to join in. Every year her class took on a project to help others, and this year they selected Julie's school.

Mr. Carlisle said, "Jenna, you know Julie really wants to run this year. Your mother and I think she can do it, but you would need to run with her. What do you think?"

Jenna hadn't been counting on that. She had been planning to do her very best at running too. She thought she could win in her age division. "Dad, do I have to? If I have to run with Julie, I won't have a chance at winning my division."

"I know that's a lot to give up. Think about it. You know how much Julie looks up to you."

Jenna talked it over with her friend. "What's the right thing to do? I really wanted to make this my best year."

"Julie's a great kid, Jenna," her friend said. "You mean a lot to her. You won't win the race, but I think it's the best thing to do."

Jenna finally agreed. She and Julie ran and walked their laps together. They didn't win a ribbon for the best time … but Jenna was the biggest money raiser!

Remember

Let us keep on running the race marked out for us.
Hebrews 12:1 NIRV

WINNERS DON'T ALWAYS HAVE TO WIN.

Take a look at some of the things you want to win. What will it cost you to win them?

Here's My Heart

Love is the fairest bloom in God's garden of character traits.

Erin carefully pasted a big red heart on the front of the card she was making. It was important that the card look just right, because it was for Grandmama, who lived in Maine.

Grandmama had been sick, and Erin hoped the card would cheer her up.

Erin's mom came into the family room and looked at the card.

"Why, Erin!" she said. "That looks just like a Valentine's Day card. But this is July!"

"I know," Erin said as she finished writing her message inside. "I was thinking about what Pastor Miles said last Sunday—how when we give our hearts to Jesus, we are promising to love him forever, the way that he will love us forever. I'm giving this heart to Grandmama so she knows that I will love her forever too."

"Anyway," Erin said, "I don't see why we can't have Valentine's Day more often. Shouldn't every day be Valentine's

Day, if you have somebody like Grandmama that you really love? I think it should."

Erin's mom smiled. *What a daughter! Every word that she said made perfect sense.*

"You're right," Mom said. "I never thought of it that way. And you know what? I bet Grandmama would like to have you tell her in person how much you love her. I think we'll plan a trip and go see her as soon as she's well."

"Great!" Erin exclaimed. "When I get to her house, I think I'll make her a heart-shaped cake."

Do everything in love.
1 Corinthians 16:14 NIV

FILL THE WORLD WITH LOVE.

We don't have to wait for special holidays to tell people how much we love them. Just like us, they like to hear it all the time. Say it today! Say it every day!

Plan B

Life is all [about] getting used to what you're not used to.

Anna and Bobby were eager to be with their grandparents for Christmas.

"I hope Papa likes the planter I made for him," Anna said. It was December 23rd, and the Chases made a list of things to be packed for the two-hour drive to their grandparents' house.

"I'm sure he will, Anna. Bobby, have you packed Grandma's gifts?" Dad asked. Bobby had decorated picture frames for their school pictures to give to Grandma. "Yes, I put everything I need in a stack. I'm ready!"

"Let's get to bed early," Mom said. As the family slept, snow began to fall. Father looked out the window when he got up. Snow covered everything! And it was still snowing.

He turned on the radio for a weather report. There was more snow to come! He called the highway department, "How are the roads to Springfield?"

The news wasn't good.

"Children," Father said, "We have to cancel our trip to Grandma and Grandpa's. The roads are really bad all the way."

Anna and Bobby were disappointed, "Now what will we do?" Father called Granddad to tell him the news, and then he went out and shoveled off the drive. At least they could get to the Christmas Eve church service.

The electricity was off at church, but it was Christmas Eve and everyone wanted to be there. It was cold and dark ... but they could still have the service. They used candles for light and everyone kept on their jackets, sweaters, hats, scarves, and mittens during the service.

"That was an adventure!" Anna said.

Bobby nodded and added, "Just like the 'olden days', huh, Dad?"

Dad laughed. "Sometimes we just have to make the most of what we can do," he said.

Remember

I have come so they can have life. I want them to
have it in the fullest possible way.
John 10:10 NIRV

LOOK FOR A SILVER LINING IN EVERY CLOUD.

You Can Do It!

When things don't turn out the way you want, then turn them around the way you can!

Follow the Signs

When we are obedient, God guides our steps and our stops.

Do Not Feed the Animals.

The sign on the wall was so big, you couldn't miss it. Even so, Meredith wanted to throw in some peanuts for the baby elephant. He looked hungry. And surely extra peanuts would help him grow to be as big as his mother, who was standing nearby.

Meredith looked around. No one was watching her. Grabbing a handful of peanuts from the bag her mom had bought for her, she got ready to throw them toward the elephants.

"Meredith!" Her mom grabbed Meredith's arm and pulled her away from the fence. "What are you doing? You know you're not supposed to feed the animals! You saw the sign."

"He looks hungry," Meredith said, wondering what kind of trouble she had just gotten herself into.

When they got home from the zoo, Meredith's mom read her a newspaper article about a zoo animal that had gotten sick because of some candy that someone had thrown into its cage.

"You see," Mom said gently, "the people at the zoo have to watch what the animals eat. The zookeepers know exactly what kind of food they can eat and how much they should have. That's why they have rules like Do Not Feed the Animals. The rules protect them."

Meredith said, "Because if they get sick, we won't be able to see them when we go to the zoo."

"Exactly," her mom said, "and we want to see that baby elephant grow up nice and healthy, don't we?"

Meredith nodded her head vigorously.

"Yes," she said. "But he'll have to eat a lot of peanuts to get as big as his mama."

Obey the laws, then, for two reasons: first, to keep from being punished, and second, just because you know you should.
Romans 13:5 TLB

FOLLOW DIRECTIONS.

It's tempting to do something that doesn't seem as if it would cause any harm, but we don't always know what's best. So when the sign says "Don't" ... don't!

The Agreement

Our differences are politics. Our agreements are principles.

Gail looked everywhere for her favorite soccer shirt—in the dresser, in the closet, under the bed, and in her old toy chest. It was nowhere to be found. She even checked her sisters' room, thinking one of them might have borrowed it, but it wasn't there either.

"Mom!" Gail finally yelled. "I can't find my shirt. You know, the blue one that I always wear to play soccer!"

A few minutes later, Gail's mom came into the bedroom, holding up the blue shirt. It was very wrinkled, and it still had some grass stains on it, as well as some mud.

"This one?" Mom asked.

"Yeah, that's it," Gail said. "Where was it? What happened to it?"

"In the laundry hamper," Mom said. "Do you remember the talk we had about doing laundry?"

Boy, did Gail remember. Mom taught her how to use the washing machine and dryer, and Gail had agreed that she would do at least one load of her clothes each week.

"You can't wear this shirt today," Mom said. "It's dirty."

"What else can I wear?" Gail asked.

Mom looked at her. She waited, and Gail realized what she needed to say.

"Okay, Mom, I know I messed up on the laundry. It's my fault the shirt is still dirty. I'll wear my red one. And I promise—from now on, I'll do my laundry. If I forget, you have my permission to remind me! It's worth it to be able to wear my favorite clothes whenever I want to."

Mom smiled approvingly.

God is at work within you, helping you want to obey him, and then helping you do what he wants.
Philippians 2:13 TLB

TAKE CARE OF YOUR THINGS.

Is doing laundry fun? It can be, if you look at it in the right way. You're washing away dirt ... the way Jesus washed away all of your sins when He died on the cross and rose again.

Clean Your Plates

It isn't the thing you do; It's the thing you leave undone, which gives you a bit of heartache at the setting of the sun.

When the dishwasher broke, Mom announced that everyone would have to take turns doing dishes until it was fixed.

Wednesday night was Kimmi's night to wash up. She stood on a stool that helped her reach the sink and started washing the plates that had been soaking.

"Kimmi! Your favorite show is coming on!" her sister called from the family room.

Kimmi looked at all the dishes to be washed and frowned at the thought of missing her TV show. Maybe she could hurry. Giving each dish, glass, and piece of silverware a quick swipe with the sponge, she rinsed them with warm water and put them into the drainer, then hopped down off the stool to go join her sister in the family room.

Right before bedtime, Kimmi's mom called her into the kitchen and held up two of the plates. Both still had some spaghetti sauce on them.

"These aren't clean," Mom said. "What happened?"

"I was in a hurry," Kimmi said. "I thought I did them right. I didn't notice the sauce."

Mom put the dishes back into the sink and turned on the water. "When you're given a job to do," she said, "always do your best. It's no fun eating from dirty dishes, is it?"

"Yuck! No!" Kimmi said.

"What do you think we should do?" Mom asked.

"I think I should wash them again," Kimmi said.

"That's a good decision," Mom said. "Remember that it's always faster to do something right the first time. I'll tell you what—you wash and I'll dry, and we'll have these done in no time."

"And they'll be nice and clean for breakfast," Kimmi said. "And tomorrow, it's Dad's turn to wash up!"

Do not be lazy but work hard
serving the Lord with all your heart.
Romans 12:11 NCV

INSPECT YOUR WORK ... BEFORE OTHERS DO!

When we do chores for others, we should remember that God is paying attention to how well we're doing them. If you remember that everything you do is really for God, that'll help you do everything better.

Shared Grandparents

[My grandmother] taught me early on about doing the right thing, working hard, doing a job well, and having fun.

"David! Abbie! Cameron! Come to the house, please!" Dad called to the children in the backyard.

It was a beautiful fall Saturday and they were enjoying the outdoors.

"Your grandparents called and need help moving their deck furniture into the garage. They'll be leaving soon for Florida for the winter, and they need to get this done. I told them we would go over this afternoon."

The kids loved their grandparents … but they had other plans. "I was going fishing with Joseph," Cameron whined.

"Angela and I were going to ride bikes this afternoon," Abbie responded.

The youngest, David, was not yet in school. "Dad, I can help. I'll do it with you!"

"Thanks, David," he said, "Now, how about you two?"

"I guess we can fish some other time," Cameron said.

Abbie was not eager to give up her bike ride, but she said, "Well, okay. I'll call Angela."

"Thanks, kids. Maybe your friends would want to join us. It won't take long."

Mr. and Mrs. Stebbins loaded the kids in the van, and on the way, they picked up Angela.

The chore only took an hour with all of them working together. Afterwards, Grandma and Grandpa had hot cider and popcorn ready. "Thanks a lot, kids," Grandpa said. "We couldn't have done it without you."

"Thank you for the popcorn and cider!" the children replied.

On the way home in the car, Angela said, "Thanks for sharing your grandparents with me. Mine live far away and I miss them. Your grandparents are a lot like mine. I had fun!"

Share with God's people who need help.
Bring strangers in need into your homes.
Romans 12:13 ICB

INCLUDE OTHERS TO HELP OTHERS.

If you see a need, ask friends and family to help. Share your joy.

The Ribbon Hangers

A [sister] is a friend provided by nature.

"Mom! She did it again!" Trish wailed. "I haven't even WORN these pants yet, and she's already worn them and torn the zipper. I was going to wear them to a party tonight!"

Trish's mom looked sympathetic. "Dolly just doesn't understand you don't want her to borrow your things. She may be as big as you, but she's younger and I think she really looks up to you. She wants to fit in with your friends, and maybe she thinks wearing your clothes will help her do that."

Trish wasn't impressed, but she let the matter drop.

Two days later, it happened again. This time Trish's mother promised to talk to Dolly.

"Trish, why don't you like me?" asked Dolly when she came into their room.

"I like you, but I don't like that you treat my things like they belong to you," said Trish.

"I'm sorry," whispered Dolly. Suddenly Dolly looked very small sitting on the bed, and Trish began to feel sorry for her.

After all, Dolly was her sister since her mom married Dolly's dad.

Trish went to her closet and found two hangers. She tied small red ribbons around the neck of each hanger and placed them in a spot that divided her half of the closet from Dolly's half.

"Dolly, this will help us respect each other's side of the closet. I won't wear anything on your side, and you won't wear anything from mine."

"What are those two ribbon hangers for?" asked Dolly.

"Well," said Trish, "if every now and then something of mine ends up on one of these hangers, it's for either of us to wear."

Trish's mom overheard the new rule, and every now and then something neither girl had ever seen before shows up on a ribbon hanger.

Love each other like brothers and sisters. Give your brothers and sisters more honor than you want for yourselves.
Romans 12:10 ICB

ACCEPT AND LOVE YOUR FAMILY.

Accept new family members as they are, and appreciate them for their differences as well as their similarities to you.

A Reason for Everything

People see God every day, they just don't recognize him.

Todd and Carrie set out with their mom for their favorite restaurant. Their dad was out of town and Mom's car was getting repaired. Mom often treated the kids to dinner out when Dad was away.

"We can walk," Todd had said. "The restaurant is only about twelve blocks away."

"Okay, kids. Let's give it a go!"

"Hurray!" Todd and Carrie shouted.

The walk took longer than they had thought, but they all stayed with it and kept on walking.

"I can see the sign. Only two more blocks and we're there, Carrie. You can do it!"

And they did! The restaurant was crowded and the order took longer than usual. But it tasted great! After dinner they started for home. It was late and Carrie was tired after the long walk there. She finally just sat down on the sidewalk and cried.

"Let's pray, kids, that we will get a ride home," Mom said.

Within minutes, a neighbor drove by and noticed the Grissoms. "Hey, do you need a ride?"

"Yes, thanks!" said Mrs. Grissom.

"Hop in."

"Mrs. Jackson, Carrie got too tired to walk home so we prayed for a ride. It wasn't long before you came along in the car," Todd said.

"Really? Is that so?" Mrs. Jackson replied.

"I can't wait to tell my Sunday school class," Todd replied. "Mrs. Jackson, do you want to come to church with us?"

Mrs. Jackson and her husband never went to church, but now she thought it might be a good idea.

"Why sure, Todd," she said. "Mr. Jackson and I would love to go with you."

Remember

"If you ask for anything in my name, I will do it for you. Then the Father's glory will be shown through the Son."
John 14:13 ICB

PRAY ABOUT EVERYTHING.

You Can Do It!

Share a prayer—and then share the answer. God will use it to bless others.

Saving Up

Pennies do not come from heaven.
They have to be earned here on earth.

When Jacey didn't get the bicycle she wanted for Christmas, she was really disappointed. Her mom noticed how quiet she was after the family finished opening presents.

"You're upset about the bike, aren't you, Jacey?" Mom asked gently.

Jacey just nodded and tried not to cry.

"We couldn't afford to get it for you," Mom said. "I have an idea though. You can save up for a bike."

"But the one I want costs $60!" Jacey protested.

"Let's set up a savings plan," Mom said. "How much money do you have in your bank?"

"Twelve dollars."

"That's twenty percent," Mom said. "You'll be earning some money for watching the Carters' cat while they're out of town next month, and there's your allowance. You could recycle our newspapers and aluminum cans, too."

After months of pet-sitting, plant-watering, household

chores, recycling, and running some errands for one of the neighbors, Jacey sat down to count her money: $55! She was still $5 short.

"I'll never get my bike," she told her mom.

"Yes, you will," Mom said. "Dad and I have been talking. We're so impressed with how hard you've worked, we want to help you." She pulled a $5 bill out of her pocket and handed it to Jacey.

"Why don't we go to the store right now?" Mom smiled. "I bet there's a bike just waiting for you."

"Thanks, Mom," Jacey said, hugging her. "This bike is going to be extra special, because I worked so hard for it. It was really worth waiting for."

Money that comes easily disappears quickly,
but money that is gathered little by little will slowly grow.
Proverbs 13:11 NCV

SAVE YOUR PENNIES. THEY
BECOME DOLLARS.

We don't always get everything we ask for, and that's good. God makes sure we have everything we need; the rest is icing on the cake!

A Bad Idea

Marshall thought the school day would never end. She had received an invitation to go to Zoey's house with a bunch of other kids to listen to music, and she had a great CD collection.

The final bell of the day rang at last. Marshall and the others rode their bikes to Zoey's. They each chose their favorite sodas from the basement refrigerator and flopped down on the over-stuffed couches and chairs. The music Zoey selected was terrific, and everyone was soon having a great time. At one point, Zoey ran upstairs and came back down with something hidden behind her back.

"Anybody want to try some of this?" she asked, showing them a bottle of wine.

"Zoey! Your mom's going to kill you!" squealed one of the kids.

"She's not home yet," Zoey said. "She called and said she'd be late."

"We still can't drink that," Marshall said.

"Why not?" Zoey demanded.

"Because," Marshall said, "we're too young, it's illegal, it's bad for us, and our parents have all told us not to."

"Our parents will never know," Zoey said.

"Yes, they will," one girl replied. "My mom always knows when I've done something wrong."

"You guys are no fun," Zoey pouted.

"What's fun about breaking the rules, getting sick, and getting caught and punished?" Marshall asked.

"Marshall's right," said one of the boys. "Doing something on purpose that could get you into trouble is just plain stupid. And as my dad says, he's not raising stupid kids."

"Okay, fine," Zoey said. "Maybe you're right. I don't want to get yelled at either."

Keep on being faithful to what you were taught and to what you believed. After all, you know who taught you these things.
2 Timothy 3:14 CEV

STAND UP FOR WHAT YOU BELIEVE.

Do what's right just because it's right. Somewhere along the way, you'll find a reward for your decision that benefits you.

A New Attitude

How many people stop because so few say, Go!

"I just know I'm going to flunk that geography test," moaned Courtney to her older cousin, Randi.

"How do you know that?" Randi asked.

"Because I'm no good at memorizing stuff."

"Have you been paying attention in class and doing all the homework?" Randi asked. "And do you always study hard for a test?"

"Yes, but it's no use," Courtney said glumly. "A boy in my class says girls are no good with maps and stuff. So it's no use. I'll fail no matter what I do."

"Wait a minute," Randi said. "You need to forget about what that boy said. Plenty of boys are bad with maps—my dad is always getting lost when we go on car trips! It sounds to me like you're doing all the right things. Maybe you just need to change your attitude."

"How?" Courtney asked.

"Tell yourself that you're smart, that you know how and what to study, and you're going to pass this test. Believe in yourself!"

"Why should I?"

"Because I do," Randi told her. "I know you can do it. Look at how good you are in other subjects."

"Maybe you're right. Maybe I am smarter than I think I am."

"You are," Randi said. "There's no maybe about it. I know that with the right attitude, you'll do great on that test. I'll even help you study for it."

"I believe you!" Courtney said, with confidence in her voice. "I'm going to start studying right now. Who says I can't get an A?"

"Not me!" laughed Randi, reaching for the geography book.

You help me defeat armies and capture cities.
Psalm 18:29 CEV

BELIEVE IN YOURSELF.

You are a child of the King. He knows everything, and he would be happy to share all his knowledge with you. And he believes in you. That's a winning combination.

Afraid? Who, Me?

Faith is not merely you holding on to God—
it is God holding on to you.

Nora was shaking all over when she got out of the car. On her last trip to the dentist, Dr. Olson had found a small cavity in one of her teeth. Today he was going to fill it.

"I'm scared, Mom," Nora said as they sat down in the waiting room. She was shivering.

"There's nothing to be afraid of," Mom said. "This will take only a few minutes."

"My friend Beth had to get a filling once, and she said it was awful."

Nora's mom took her hand. "Remember how you were afraid of the water until you learned how to swim? That was because you didn't know what to expect. Remember how we prayed before you took that first swimming lesson?"

"Yeah," Nora said. "It turned out okay, because I had a good teacher who was really nice."

"You like Dr. Olson, right?"

"Yes. He always calls me 'Nora from Bora Bora.' He makes me laugh."

"I have an idea," Mom said. "Let's pray right now and ask God to take away your fear." They bowed their heads as Nora's mom prayed.

Thirty minutes later, Nora had gone in, gotten her filling, and come back out to meet her mom.

"How was it?" Mom asked.

"It was okay!" Nora said happily. "He numbed the tooth, and I didn't feel a thing. He was singing some silly song, and he was done before I knew it."

"So the prayer worked?" Mom asked.

"Yes," Nora nodded. "And it felt good to know that God was in there with me the whole time."

The Lord gives me light and saves me. Why should I fear anyone?
Psalm 27:1 NIRV

HAVE NO FEAR. GOD IS HERE!

Going to the doctor or the dentist doesn't have to be scary. God is always going to go with you. Just ask him to hold your hand. He can take away your fear.

Taking a Collection

Trust God for great things. With your five loaves and two fishes, He will show you a way to feed thousands.

It was a few weeks after Alston and his twin sister, Adela, had returned to school following summer vacation. Alston looked at the calendar and became depressed.

"What's wrong with you?" asked Adela, who noticed that he seemed unhappy.

"It's two whole months until Thanksgiving," Alston said gloomily, "and three whole months until Christmas. I know we have that All Saints party at church in November, but I need something to think about now besides just school, homework, and tests."

"Let me see that calendar," Adela said. She had to admit, there wasn't much happening until after October.

"Do you realize how the two of you sound?" their mother asked. "All you can think about are holidays! You need to think about something else."

"Like what?" asked Alston.

"Like other people. If you really want something to do in October, why don't you do something for World Food Day? It's on October 16. It's to remind people like us that there are lots of people in the world who are starving."

"What can we do?" asked Adela.

"Maybe you can collect canned goods for the local food bank," Mom said.

Alston thought for a minute. "We could tell the people at church what we're doing and ask them to bring stuff on Sundays."

"Maybe the principal would let us make an announcement at school," Adela suggested.

"I bet our neighbors would help, too," said Alston.

Mom offered, "Dad and I can help pick up and deliver the food."

Remember

When you help the poor you are lending to the Lord—
and he pays wonderful interest on your loan!
Proverbs 19:17 TLB

HELP FEED THE HUNGRY.

Instead of thinking about fun things that you can do for yourself, take time now and then to think about things you can do for others. Lots of people need help.

Good Manners Matter

Politeness goes far, yet costs nothing.

As a special treat for her birthday, Sonia's parents took her out to dinner at a very nice restaurant. There were white tablecloths and flowers and candles and extra-shiny silverware on every table.

Sonia put her napkin in her lap the way she saw her mom do it and thanked the waiter who poured her a glass of water. When she placed her order, she copied her dad's style: "May I please have the lasagna and a green salad with Italian dressing?" The waiter smiled and wrote it down.

At the next table, Sonia noticed another family with two children. The boy was pouring salt and pepper on the tablecloth and the girl knocked over the vase of flowers, spilling water everywhere.

"Behave, you two!" the mother said, but they ignored her. She just shook her head, sighed, and went back to talking to her husband.

When their food came, Sonia and her parents thanked the waiter. The boy at the next table yelled for the waiter to come refill his soda glass.

Sonia's family finished their meal and agreed that it had been delicious. The waiter brought the check. "It has been a pleasure serving you," he said, looking over his shoulder at the other table. "I really mean that."

Sonia's dad smiled at his daughter after the waiter left. "And it's a pleasure for me to have a daughter with such good manners."

"Amen!" Sonia's mother agreed. "Let's go home and dig into that birthday cake, shall we?"

Show respect for everyone.
1 Peter 2:17 TLB

MIND YOUR MANNERS.

God has perfect manners. He doesn't yell or scream or force us to do things. It's a pleasure to serve him.

❋ Which Will It Be? ❋

You have to make your own choices, And then you live with them.

Sonji started clarinet lessons in second grade, and she learned how to read music. All those dots and lines on the music sheet started to make sense. Learning the fingering for each note was hard, but she was getting better. Most important, the "squeaking" sounds of her first lessons began to disappear.

Sonji had wanted to play clarinet for a long time. She asked her mom and dad if she could get one. First they rented one, then when she continued to practice, they bought one for her.

But after two years of clarinet lessons, she began to cut practice time short. She wasn't exactly losing interest, it was just that there were other things she wanted to do … like gymnastics.

Her parents set limits on the number of after-school activities during the school year. She was in Girl Scouts, took clarinet lessons, and spent one night a week with the kids in her church youth group. There wasn't any extra time for gymnastics lessons, unless she gave up something else.

Sonji wasn't one to do things halfway. If she was going to take part, she wanted to make her best effort. She talked it over with her parents, but it was up to Sonji to make the decision. Either gymnastics or clarinet. How would she choose?

Sonji prayed for wisdom to make the choice. Then she announced her decision to her parents—she would continue the clarinet lessons.

"What made you choose the clarinet?" Dad asked.

Sonji said, "I can take some gymnastics in physical education class at school. And I think I'm going to be able to play the clarinet a lot longer than I could do gymnastics competitions."

"Good choice!" Mom said.

Lord, I trust you. I have said, "You are my God."
My life is in your hands.
Psalm 31:14–15 ICB

GOD CARES ABOUT EVERY DETAIL.

Pray about your choices, and then decide with confidence that your prayer has been heard and answered.

❋ Honor Your Parents ❋

He who says what he likes, often hears
in reply what he does not like.

Mishi, Nia, and their dad were invited to a Fourth of July cookout at Micah's house. About ten families came to enjoy the sunshine, the pool, and some good food.

As the afternoon wore on, some of the dads played horseshoes while the kids played tag and the moms made sure the food and ice didn't run out.

Micah, who was hot and sweaty from running, came dashing up to his mom and demanded a popsicle.

"Just a minute," his mom said. "I need to finish dishing out this salad."

"Now!" Micah demanded. "I want a popsicle now, not later!"

"Keep your voice down," Micah's mom said.

"No!" Micah yelled, stomping his foot. "Get it for me now!"

Micah's mom gave him a look and told him to go with her into the house. She returned a few minutes later and said that Micah would be staying in his room for a while.

Mishi and Nia talked about what had happened as their dad drove them home a couple of hours later.

"Poor Micah missed the rest of the party," Mishi said.

"I think she should have just yelled at him!" Nia exclaimed.

"Or given him the popsicle," Mishi said.

"Do you think Micah deserved the popsicle?" Dad asked. "It seems to me he was being very disrespectful."

"But it was a party!" Mishi said. "And he was hot."

"That doesn't give anyone the right to be disrespectful or rude," Dad said. "You should always be polite to other people—especially your parents. If you can't respect the most important people in your life, you'll never learn how to respect strangers. And believe me, showing respect will make you a lot more popular than being rude."

"And you'll spend less time in your room," Nia said.

Honor your father and mother, just as the Lord your God commanded you. Then you will live a long time in the land he is giving you. And things will go well with you there.
Deuteronomy 5:16 NIRV

RESPECT BRINGS GREAT REWARDS.

When is the best time to honor your parents and show proper respect for them? All the time! There is no "time off" from treating your parents the way God expects you to treat them. Be respectful!

Winner ... and Still Champion*

When one door of happiness closes, another opens; but often we look so long at the closed door that we do not see the one which has been opened to us.

Dierdre had always dreamed of being a figure skater. Posters of Olympic women figure skaters hung all over her room. Mom and Dad encouraged Dierdre's dream. She took skating lessons and even ballet and gymnastics to become strong and graceful. Dierdre knew it meant hard work to become a good skater.

Now it was winter and the perfect time for outdoor skating. Dierdre had a cold, but that was not unusual. Then the head cold became joint and muscle aches. Next, a virus settled in her back and spinal cord. Her temperature was over 103 degrees. Dierdre lost feeling in her feet and legs.

"Will I be able to skate again?" she asked the doctor.

"We'll see," she responded. "All of the training you did will help."

After days and weeks of physical therapy, Dierdre improved, but she did not have a full recovery. What she had been able to do easily and gracefully before she became ill was now painful and awkward.

"Mom, Dad, I really want to be a skater. I don't know if I'll ever be able to ..." and she burst into tears.

"Dierdre, we know something good can come of this. Let's pray that it will. You are giving it your very best effort. We're so proud of you."

Dierdre's hard work at physical therapy earned her the respect of her physical therapist. "Dierdre," he said, "we won't know for a while if you'll be able to skate again like you once did. But I know something you can do now."

"What's that?" she asked.

"There's a little girl in my afternoon physical therapy class who injured her back in gymnastics. Would you talk to her? She's discouraged and needs someone to look up to who can help her face this disappointment."

Suddenly Dierdre felt strong and useful.

Remember

I can do all things though Christ because he gives me strength.
Philippians 4:13 ICB

DISAPPOINTMENTS CONTAIN
UNEXPECTED BLESSINGS.

You Can Do It!

Write down a disappointment you've experienced in your life. How has it made you a better, stronger person?

Let's Make a Plan

The glory of friendship is ... the spiritual inspiration that comes to one when he discovers that someone else believes in him and is willing to trust him.

Alyssa had enjoyed her neighbor Mrs. Parks ever since she could remember. She stopped at her house every Wednesday after school for "tea time."

Mrs. Parks was the most fascinating person Alyssa had ever met. She knew everything there was to know. And if she didn't know it, she would study it. Mrs. Parks taught Alyssa how to roll a pie crust, how to make up a hospital bed, and how to fix a bicycle tire. They even went fishing and cleaned the fish they caught.

Mrs. Parks was always learning new things. Alyssa could talk to her about anything ... and she did. She told Mrs. Parks that her parents argued a lot. It had been hard at home since Alyssa's father lost his job at the airlines.

"Alyssa," Mrs. Parks said, "let's think of a way we can help your mother and father. Making ends meet must be really hard for them right now."

"I don't know what to do," Alyssa said, close to tears.

"Let's have a giant garage sale," suggested Mrs. Parks. "You can make some money for your family. We'll go around the neighborhood and collect things people no longer want and then sell them on commission. We'll give them 40 percent of the price we get paid for the item."

"Great idea, and I have some Rollerblades that are too small and some kids' videos that I no longer watch."

"Sounds like we have a plan that will work. Now let's ask your parents."

The two went to Alyssa's house and told them their idea. They all agreed—and they all worked together to have a very successful garage sale!

As iron sharpens iron, so one person sharpens another.
Proverbs 27:17 NIRV

FRIENDS CAN BE PART OF THE SOLUTION.

Involve others in working out ways to help those in need.

Do Not Enter

The way out of trouble is never as simple
as the way in.

The warehouse on the outskirts of town had been boarded up for years. There were padlocks on all the doors and No Trespassing signs everywhere. Jackson and Amber passed it every day on their way to school.

Jackson and his sister were new in town. They moved to Sundale in early August. Eager to fit in, they were happy when K.J., one of the boys in Jackson's class, asked them to walk home from school with him and his friends.

As they approached the warehouse, K.J. said, "I know a way to get in there. Let's go check it out."

"Yeah, let's do it," said Terese.

"But the signs say 'No Trespassing,'" Amber protested.

"You're not afraid, are you?" one of the boys teased her.

"We'd be breaking the law," Jackson said, defending his sister.

"There're no cops around," Bobby offered. "No one will know."

"We'll all know we did something wrong," Amber said.

"I'm going in," said K.J. "Anybody else coming?"

"Sure, I'm not scared," said Bobby, making a face at Amber. Everyone except Jackson and Amber went with him.

Moments later, alarms went off. Jackson and Amber watched as five scared kids were escorted out of the building by a security guard who patrolled the lot. "No! Don't call my parents!" they heard Terese cry.

"I'm glad we didn't go in there," Amber said as they headed home.

"Me too," said Jackson. "I want to make friends, but not the kind who will get us into trouble."

A person who calls himself a Christian should not be
doing things that are wrong.
2 Timothy 2:19 TLB

TURN AWAY FROM TROUBLE.

As a Christian, God wants you to set a good example for other people. You can be a leader. You can stand up for what's right, no matter how old you are.

Rainy-Day Project

"Mom, I don't have anything to do. It's raining outside and I'm bored," moaned LeeAnn.

"I need some help making lasagna for tonight. Our community group is serving dinner at the homeless shelter. It's our family's turn to take a meal. Can you help me?" Mother asked.

"I'm good at stirring and chopping."

"Get out the recipe and let's check to see if we have all the ingredients we need."

LeeAnn read the ingredients aloud while Mom checked the cupboards. "Tomatoes and tomato paste, lasagna noodles, hamburger, spices, cheese, eggs, onions ... "

"We don't have any onions," Mom said. "I'll call Mrs. Ross and see if she has some I can borrow. Then you can run over and get them."

Mrs. Ross, their neighbor, met LeeAnn at the door with several onions. "What are you making?" she asked.

"We're making lasagna to take to the homeless shelter for dinner tonight. We didn't have any onions."

192

"Do you need anything else?" Mrs. Ross asked. "I can make a cake for dessert."

"I'm sure they can always use more," said LeeAnn. "We'll take it down when we go to serve."

"I'll be glad to help."

The afternoon went by fast with all the cooking and baking. The food was all ready to go by four o'clock. Dad came home and they stopped by Mrs. Ross' house for the cake, and then drove down to the shelter.

After dinner, LeeAnn found a corner where the youngest children played. "I'll read to the little children," LeeAnn said, "while their moms wash clothes."

The Andersons were all tired when they got home. But they all agreed they wanted to help again.

Share with God's people who are in need.
Romans 12:13 NIRV

GOD WANTS TO DO HIS WORK THROUGH YOU!

Ask God what you can do. You're never too young or too old to do something nice for others.

Rollerblading Buddies ❋

Sports do not build character,

they reveal it.

All the girls brought their Rollerblades, helmets, and knee and elbow pads to girls' club. This afternoon they were headed to River Parks to Rollerblade.

Carlie was new to Rollerblades. She had just received a pair for a birthday present two weeks before.

"Watch where you're going, girls," said their leader, Mrs. Vance, "and we'll see you back here in an hour."

"I've done this trail dozens of times," said Carlie's friend Patricia. "I know it well."

And with that, the girls were off.

"Watch this!" Patricia yelled as she took one of the jumps along the trail.

"You're good, Patricia!"

"You are going too slow. I'm going to catch the leader." Patricia said as she wove in and out of the Rollerbladers—something they weren't supposed to do. But Patricia was probably the best skater in girls' club. She could stop fast if she needed to.

"Coming from your left," she called out as she passed a group of girls. She turned to wave as she sped by.

"Watch out!" the girls yelled.

What Patricia hadn't seen was a group of bicyclists coming up the hill from the opposite direction. They collided head-on. Bikes and Rollerblades were everywhere.

"Hey, watch out next time!" shouted one of the bikers.

"I'm sorry. I'm so sorry," Patricia cried as she picked herself up from the heap.

"You were just showing off!" shouted another biker.

By this time Carlie had caught up. "Patricia, are you okay?"

"Yes, but barely," Patricia said. "I need to watch where I'm going instead of hoping other people will watch me."

Be very careful how you live. Do not live like people who aren't wise. Live like people who are wise.
Ephesians 5:15 NIRV

CARELESS BEHAVIOR CAUSES INJURY.

Obey the rules of safe conduct. They are to protect you and others too.

Someone Worth Copying

Nurture your minds with great thoughts.
To believe in the heroic makes heroes.

The funeral for Madison's grandfather was one of the biggest the town had ever seen. More than 500 people came to the church for the memorial service. Friends of Granddad who had known him since childhood, neighbors, people he'd worked with, younger friends, shopkeepers, siblings, his children, and his grandchildren—they all came to celebrate the life he had lived. Madison had no idea her granddad had known so many people!

"We're here today to say good-bye to a dear friend," the minister said as the service began. "The good news is, it's not really good-bye; it's more like 'See you later, Floyd,' because we know Floyd is in heaven with our Lord, and we know we'll see him again when we all get there."

When the minister finished speaking, several of Granddad's friends and relatives got up to talk about how special he had been. They told story after story about the times he had loaned them money, helped shovel snow from their driveways, jump-started their cars, gave them rides to the airport, comforted them when their loved ones died—it seemed as if Granddad had stopped at nothing to show God's love to the people in his life.

"The best thing I can say about my dad," Madison's dad added, "is that I am a better person because my dad was a loving, compassionate, honest, forgiving man, and I always wanted to be just like him."

"You know what, Dad?" Madison said when the service ended. "After hearing all those people say all those great things about Granddad, I've decided that I want to be just like him too."

Follow God's example in everything you do
just as a much loved child imitates his father.
Ephesians 5:1 TLB

JESUS IS THE BEST EXAMPLE TO FOLLOW.

It's wonderful to try to be like people who are setting a good example for us. The best example we've ever had is Jesus. If we can be like him, we will really be something!

The Debut

Share your courage with others.

Millie peered through the curtain at the edge of the stage and felt a huge lump develop immediately in her throat. The school auditorium was packed, and people were standing in the back.

"Do we have a crowd?" Keri asked.

"A big one," Millie said. "I feel kinda sick."

"You'll be great!" Keri said. "You have a beautiful voice and you know your song. You were perfect last night in dress rehearsal."

"There wasn't an audience at dress rehearsal," Millie moaned.

"You'll be wonderful!" Keri said with even greater enthusiasm.

"You've done this lots of times before, Keri," Millie said. "This is my first time to have a solo."

"Well, I'll tell you what," Keri said. "I'm standing in the chorus right behind you. If you forget the words, I'll come sing harmony with you. If you faint, I'll step out and sing the rest of your song."

Millie laughed. "Why don't you just do that anyway?"

Keri said, "Naw. This is your night to shine. But I'll tell you what works for me—sing to the back wall. Don't look down into the lights, and don't look into the first few rows of the audience."

"Thanks," Millie said. "That's what Miss Beecher said too."

"Hey, that's our cue!" Keri said. And before she knew it, Millie hurried to get in line for their entrance. As they stood in line, Keri turned around and gave her one more big grin and a thumbs-up sign. Millie smiled back and thought, *What a great thing to have a friend who isn't afraid to share the spotlight ... or her courage!*

Encourage the timid.
1 Thessalonians 5:14 TEV

ENCOURAGE SOMEONE TODAY.

To encourage is to put your courage into another person. Do you know someone who is afraid? Do what you can to encourage that person!

Kindness Counts

The only time to look down on your neighbor
is when you are bending over to help.

Daphne and Gregory were in the backyard playing bad-minton. Their mom had asked them to go outside and play while she finished some reports from her office.

A few minutes after the two of them started their game, Clifton from next door came through the gate.

"Hi!" he said.

"Not him again," Gregory muttered under his breath.

For once, Daphne agreed with her brother.

"Hi, Clifton," she said. "I'm really sorry, but Gregory and I have to go in now. Our mom needs us to do something for her. We'll see you later." She and Gregory walked away. Clifton stood alone in the yard, looking very sad.

Mom was standing at the sink when Daphne and Gregory came in.

"Why didn't you invite Clifton to come in?" she asked.

"He's always coming over," Daphne complained.

"I'm tired of playing with him," Gregory added.

"I think you should be nicer to him," Mom said. "You know that his parents are getting a divorce. Clifton doesn't know which one of them he will be living with. I think he's probably lonely and confused and feeling unloved. I think he could really use a friend or two right now."

Daphne and Gregory felt ashamed of their behavior.

"Let's ask Clifton to come over for dinner, okay?" Mom asked.

"Okay," Daphne agreed. "Can we make some brownies for dessert? I know he likes those."

"And after dinner," Gregory said, "Clifton and I can play with those walkie-talkies Dad gave me for my birthday."

Remember

It is a sin to hate your neighbor, but being kind to the needy brings happiness.
Proverbs 14:21 NCV

KINDNESS COUNTS.

How do you think Jesus would treat your next-door neighbor? Treat your neighbors the way Jesus would treat them. If you think it's hard to do, ask him to help you show them his love.

Feeding Tigger

All creatures great and small ... the Lord
God made them all.

"Have you fed Tigger?" Mom asked. Tigger was the family cat—a large striped tabby the family had picked up at the animal shelter a few weeks ago. Tigger had purred her way into the lap, and heart, of every family member since then. She was a sweet, lovable animal.

"I'll do it later," Angelina said. "I'm watching a show." Angelina barely looked up from the TV as she spoke.

"Please feed Tigger now," Mom said. "It's six o'clock."

"Can't it wait just a few more minutes?" Angelina said.

"No," Mom replied. "We agreed that Tigger would be fed before supper. Animals need to be able to count on their food at certain times."

"All right," Angelina said. Tigger was becoming a little more of a bother than she had counted on. Mom even expected her to empty the litter box and brush Tigger each day. "I guess I have to do everything," Angelina sighed.

Mom said, "Angie, let's talk a minute. You were the one who begged to have a cat. You were the one who chose Tigger at the shelter. You were the one who said, 'I'll take care of her'—even after we told you what that meant. You are the one who insists that Tigger is your cat. When God gives us an animal to take care of, he expects us to take care of it, not ignore it."

"I know," Angelina said. "It's just a lot of work."

"Everything we love," Mom said, "takes work—including our relationships with every person we love." She then got up and gave Angelina a hug as she said, "The way you take care of Tigger today is going to prepare you for taking care of other people some-day—maybe even a daughter!"

Whoever is faithful in small matters will be faithful in large ones.
Luke 16:10 TEV

BEING FAITHFUL BUILDS CHARACTER.

When you take care of a pet or do a chore regularly, without being told to do it, you are showing self-discipline. That is one of the most important character traits you can ever develop.

A Coating of Love

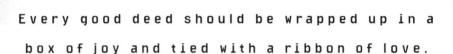

Every good deed should be wrapped up in a box of joy and tied with a ribbon of love.

———— ✱ ————

"What have you been doing?" Aunt Jen asked her niece Skyler, who seemed especially sweaty and dirty.

"Chalking up a batch of good deeds," Skyler said. "My youth group and I were out along the highway with the youth pastor picking up trash and aluminum cans. One group picked up the cans so we can recycle them. Another group picked up paper trash and other garbage. It was pretty gross."

"Good deeds, huh?"

"Yeah," Skyler said. "The way I figure it, I got lots of points in heaven today."

"Oh?" said Aunt Jen. "Do you think good deeds translate into heavenly rewards?"

"Well, don't they?" Skyler asked.

"I like the approach of a woman I read about just last week," said Aunt Jen. "Her name was Mother Teresa, and she worked with very poor and very sick and dying people in India."

"That would be lots of good points!" Skyler said.

"Mother Teresa was asked about heaven one day and this is what she said," Aunt Jen said as she reached for a book and opened it to read this quote: "I am not sure exactly what heaven will be like, but I do know that when we die and it comes time for God to judge us, He will not ask, 'How many good things have you done in your life?' Rather, He will ask, 'How much love did you put into what you did?'"

Skyler stared at Aunt Jen for a few seconds. "I guess most of what I did today was without love, but next week …"

God is love, and whoever lives in love lives in union
with God and God lives in union with him.
1 John 4:16 TEV

DO EVERYTHING WITH A LOVING HEART.

How can you put love into everything you do? By doing every good deed as if you were doing it to show your love to Jesus.

The Cookies

There is no danger of developing eyestrain from looking on the bright side.

William and his friend Rena were really enjoying their snow day. Rena went to William's house that morning to build a snowman. William's mom gave them an old stocking cap, gloves, a scarf, and a carrot for the nose. Both children were convinced their creation was the best snowman they'd ever seen.

William's mom called them inside for hot chocolate and freshly baked sugar cookies. This was turning out to be an absolutely great day.

"My mom never bakes cookies," Rena said. "We always have the store-bought kind. And she would never give me stuff to dress a snowman."

"Your mom works downtown, doesn't she?" asked William's mom.

"Yes," said Rena.

"I bet she has to get up really early to go to work," William guessed.

"Yeah, she's always gone before I leave for school. My brother has to take me to the bus stop."

"It was neat when she came and talked to our class about being a lawyer," William said. "That's what I want to be someday."

"I forgot about that," Rena said. "But I wish she was home more."

"I'm sure she'd rather spend more time with you and your brother," William's mom said, "but I always see her at your school plays. And she went with you on that class trip last month."

"I know," sighed Rena. "She does lots of neat stuff for me, like singing me to sleep at night. But I wish she baked cookies like these!"

"Who says you can't bake some for her?" William's mom asked. "I think she'd really like that."

"All right!" William said. "I'll get the chocolate chips."

We know how much God loves us because
we have felt his love.
1 John 4:16 TLB

TAKE THE LEAD IN SHOWING LOVE.

People who love us have lots going on in their lives, so they might not always do what we want them to do. That doesn't mean they don't love us and it shouldn't stop us from doing loving things for them.

Willing to Ask

One of the greatest pieces of economic wisdom is to know what you do not know.

"What do we have here?" Great-grandma asked as Kaylee showed her a handheld computer game.

"A game, Granny," Kaylee said. "It's my favorite game."

"Can two people play it?" Granny asked.

"No, just one," Kaylee said.

"I see," Granny said. "Do you think it's a game I should learn to play?"

"It's fun. I think you'd like to play it," Kaylee said.

"Will you show me how?" Granny asked. Kaylee quickly said yes and began to show her great-grandmother which buttons to push.

Kaylee's mother and her great-aunt Lottie dried dishes in the kitchen and listened to Granny and Kaylee talk and laugh in the dining room. Great-aunt Lottie was Granny's older sister.

"She's been like that all her life," Lottie said. "I think it's the secret to why she always has something new to talk about and why people of all ages like her so much."

"What secret are you talking about?" Kaylee's mom asked.

"From the time she was a little girl, my sister was never afraid to ask questions. She was curious about everything," Lottie said. "She'd ask people of all ages, backgrounds, and professions question after question."

"Lots of kids ask questions," Mom said.

"Yes," Lottie said, "but the difference between lots of children and my sister is that my sister would wait to hear the answers! If she didn't understand the answer, she'd ask another question and listen to another answer."

Lottie continued, "I said to her one time, 'Don't you know enough by now to get through the rest of your life.' She said, 'I don't know if I know enough. I don't know everything.' I always thought that was one of the smartest things I ever heard anyone say—and it was my eight-year-old sister saying it."

Love wisdom, and she will make you great.
Embrace her, and she will bring you honor.
Proverbs 4:8 TEV

WISDOM IS GETTING GOD'S ANSWERS.

Six of the best questions you can ask are: Who? What? When? Where? Why? and How? Don't just ask—listen to the answers!

Comfort

To ease another's heartache is to forget
one's own.

"I didn't make it," Carla said softly as Dad put his arm around her shoulder. "Maybe next year, sweetie," he said. "Freshmen hardly ever make the varsity cheerleading squad."

"I know," Carla said, "but I thought I had a real chance."

"I saw you practicing yesterday before tryouts, and I thought you had a really good chance too," Dad said. Then he teased, "But secretly, just between you and me, I didn't like the idea that all those junior and senior boys would be staring at you in a short cheerleading outfit."

Carla smiled. She knew Dad was trying to make her feel better—and actually, it was working a little. Then Carla and Dad stopped in their walk to the car. Just ahead of them was Carla's cousin Marti sitting in her car. Her head and hands were on the steering wheel, and she was sobbing so hard her whole body was shaking.

"Marti didn't make it either, Dad," Carla said.

"Maybe you'd better go talk to her."

"What will I say?"

210

"I don't know," Dad said. "Ask God to help you. Not making the cheerleading squad must be really tough for Marti. Her two older sisters were both cheerleaders and so was her mother when she was in high school. In fact, both of her older sisters were head cheerleaders. Marti is going to be a senior so she doesn't have another chance."

"I hadn't thought about all that," Carla said. "Her situation must be a whole lot harder than mine. Will you wait for me?"

"Sure," Dad said.

"Wait and pray!" Carla called out, as she walked to the passenger side of her older cousin's car, opened the door, and slid in.

Remember

You must all have the same attitude and the same feelings; love one another ... and be kind and humble with one another.
1 Peter 3:8 TEV

FEEL WHAT OTHERS ARE FEELING.

People are usually sad because they have lost someone they love or something they value very highly. Always reach out in kindness to those who are sad.

Truth or Opinion

We can be right without being
self-righteous.

"But it's the truth!" Georgina cried.

"It may have been the truth, but you didn't need to say it," her sister Lenora said.

"We're supposed to speak the truth," Georgina said and then shrugged her shoulders as if to say, *If other people don't like it, too bad.*

"We're also supposed to be loving," Lenora said. "You came across as arrogant and self-righteous. When you talk like that, nobody wants to change and do what's right. They just write you off as a kook."

"That's their problem," Georgina said, becoming even more defensive. "I just call it the way I see it. Deanna's clothes are way too short—top and bottom. She shows way too much skin. She wears way too much makeup. And you know it's true, Lee!"

Just then a small group of four very pretty Amish girls walked into the store. Their hair was pulled neatly back into white bonnets; their clothing was plain blue with white aprons, long sleeves, high necklines, and long skirts. They wore no makeup.

Lenora looked at her sister. "Ever feel like you're exposing way too much skin and wearing way too much makeup?"

Georgina looked down. "The good news for you," Lenora whispered, "is that I don't think those girls are going to leave this store and spread the word. They probably know that to criticize the faults of another person is just as wrong sometimes as having the fault."

"First take the log out of your own eye, and then you will be able to see clearly to take the speck out of your brother's eye."
Matthew 7:5 TEV

DON'T CRITICIZE OTHERS.

You can know right from wrong without judging a person as good or bad. You can speak up for what is right without putting down a person who is wrong. Try it!

Kammi's Decision

Be slow of tongue and quick of eye.

Kammi gathered up the photos for the school paper. Everyone was gone except Mrs. Compton, her advisor.

Watching from the window for her aunt's car, she noticed her friend Clarissa at the far side of the school parking lot. Clarissa had been acting weird lately—surfing the Internet and spending hours in chat rooms. Clarissa seemed lonely since her mom had started working really late nights.

Last week Clarissa said she had met someone online. His name was Franklin, and she said she felt she could talk to him about anything. But when Kammi and others teased her about having a new boyfriend, Clarissa clammed up and told them to mind their own business.

It's odd, thought Kammi. *Clarissa was supposed to be at our school paper meeting, but she wasn't. And now, there she is in the parking lot.*

Just then a car drove up and stopped by Clarissa. A man—not a boy—got out of the driver's side and walked around toward Clarissa.

Kammi watched as they talked for a few seconds. Finally, the man opened the car door and Clarissa reluctantly got into the car.

Something just didn't look right to Kammi. What should she do? Be both a busybody and a snitch as well? Clarissa's mother would be furious to know she was "dating" behind her back. If she told, it could end her friendship and she could become known as the school blabbermouth.

Kammi made a quick decision.

"Mrs. Compton, I just saw something that didn't look right."

Kammi's quick action possibly saved Clarissa's life. Franklin was wanted by the police. When Clarissa returned to school three days later, everyone was relieved to see her, and Clarissa was grateful that she had a "snoopy" friend.

There are many ways in which God works in our lives, but it is the same God who does the work in and through all of us who are his.
1 Corinthians 12:6 TLB

WATCH OUT FOR YOUR FRIENDS.

Helping to keep a friend safe is worth the risk of being called a snoop. Pray for your friends every day.

Singing with Joy

Too many develop every talent except the most vital one of all, the talent to use their talents ... willpower.

"Did you have a good time at choir tonight?" Mom asked as Helene and her next-door friend, Olivia, climbed into the back-seat of the car.

"Great!" Helene said. "We learned a new song that has hand motions. It's fun to sing, but I've really got to practice. I kept making mistakes."

Mom smiled. Helene loved to sing ... but she didn't always sing on key. She loved to dance ... but she wasn't very coordinated. Mostly Helene loved the Lord and loved to sing in the choir. Mom also knew that Helene would practice with her every night between now and Sunday morning, and that by Sunday, she'd do just fine. What Helene lacked in talent she made up for in willpower and enthusiasm.

Olivia sat quietly as Helene began to sing the new song for Mom. *What a contrast,* Mom thought. Olivia had a great deal of musical talent—a beautiful voice and a very good sense of

rhythm. Mom knew that Olivia would also have very little diffi-
culty learning the hand motions. But Olivia had no enthusiasm
for music—no desire to practice, and little desire to perform.

"Olivia, what do you think about the new song?" Mom asked.

"It's all right," Olivia shrugged. "I don't think I'm going to
church this Sunday. My mother said it would be okay if I stayed
home and caught up on some of my sleep."

"No, you've got to sing!" Helene said. "You can watch that ol'
video you want to see some other time."

Aha … the truth comes out, Mom thought. "We all have
choices to make, Olivia. We just have to make sure we make the
right choices when it comes to using our talents to bring pleasure
to God."

[Jesus said,] "Don't hide your light! Let it shine for all."
Matthew 5:15 TLB

USE THE TALENTS GOD GAVE YOU.

*Everybody is good at some-
thing. Find out what you are
good at doing, and then develop that ability. Practice that
skill, and give away your talent to bless other people.*

217

Time to Forgive

When you forgive, you in no way change the past—but you sure do change the future.

Sherrie was hurt that LeeAnn had invited a group of girls to go to the movie with her and her mom, but hadn't invited her. "I thought we were friends!" Sherrie said to her Aunt Tandy. "LeeAnn invited five girls! None of them help her with her homework or cover up for her when she doesn't want her mom to know what's going on."

"I see," said Aunt Tandy. "The problem, is that you may know too much. LeeAnn probably didn't want you opening your mouth so her mom would find out something LeeAnn didn't want her to know."

"Whatever … " Sherrie said in disgust. "I'm not going to be her friend anymore."

"No," said Aunt Tandy. "Now's the time to be the best friend LeeAnn ever had. Do you know what a really great friend does?"

"What?"

"The first thing is that they refuse to lie, cheat, or cover up. It's time LeeAnn did her own homework and faced up to the consequences of her own behavior. And there's a second thing."

"What's that?"

"A really great friend forgives."

"But LeeAnn doesn't deserve my forgiveness," Sherrie said. "And she sure hasn't asked for it."

"No, but Sherrie, nobody deserves forgiveness—not really. And no, LeeAnn probably won't ask for forgiveness. But that's not what forgiveness is all about. Forgiveness is when you put a person into God's hands and you say, to God, 'Here, You deal with her. Please help me get over this and go on with my life.'"

"That's tough to do," Sherrie said.

"But it's the right thing to do," Aunt Tandy replied. "Now, why don't we go see a movie and have dinner? Girls' night out—just you and me."

You must forgive one another just as the Lord has forgiven you.
Colossians 3:13 TEV

GIVE FORGIVENESS FREELY.

One of the best gifts you can ever give to a person is forgiveness. Is there somebody you need to forgive today?

When You Give...

Blessed are those who can give without remembering, and take without forgetting.

"I am so embarrassed," Lori said as she plopped her books onto the kitchen table.

"How can you possibly be embarrassed this early in the morning?" Lori's older sister, Renee, asked.

"Today is Shelly's birthday, and I totally forgot. I don't have a present for her. I don't even have a card, and she's going to be here for car pool in a half hour!"

"Why are you so bothered by that?" Renee asked. "After all, I don't remember Shelly giving you anything on your birthday."

"I think she did," said Lori. "But maybe not. If she didn't, I guess it's okay that I don't have anything for her. Do you remember, Mom, if Shelly gave me a birthday present on my last birthday?"

Her mom, who had been listening to the conversation while pretending to read the morning newspaper said, "Your grand-mother taught me a good lesson about giving when I was about your age."

"What did she say?" Lori asked.

"She said there were three rules when it came to giving. Rule number one was to always remember the nice things that people give to you and do for you. Rule number two was to always forget the nice things that you give to others or do for them. Rule number three was, if you forget the nice things others do for you, think up nice things you think they might have done for you!"

"That makes it even worse!" Lori exclaimed.

"No," said Mom. "There's still time. Do you remember that bath set of soaps and scrubs you were saving for the 'spa' we are planning to have as a party next month?"

"Yes!" said Lori. "Great idea, Mom! I can give her that."

"I'll get a gift bag and card," her mom said.

Remember

"When you do a kindness to someone, do it secretly—don't tell your left hand what your right hand is doing."
Matthew 6:3 TLB

REFUSE TO KEEP SCORE.

You Can Do It!

Give because you love, not because you expect a gift in return.

You Can Be a World Changer

He who influences the thought of his times
influences the times that follow.

She was just ten years old when she began to worry about the possibility of nuclear war between her country (the USA) and the Soviet Union. So Samantha Smith decided to write letters to both the Soviet and U.S. presidents. It was 1982 and Samantha was an average 5th-grader in Maine.

Samantha didn't know the Presidents had received her letters until she was called to the principal's office one day. Thinking she must have done something wrong, she was very surprised to learn that she had a telephone call from a reporter who learned that the Soviet president was trying to find Samantha to invite her to his nation. Not only did Samantha go, she suggested that the Soviet and U.S. presidents exchange granddaughters for two weeks every year because she felt that neither president would want to send a bomb to a country where his granddaughter might visit! Although her suggestion may not have been taken, Samantha nevertheless became recognized as a worldwide representative for peace.

Sadly, in August 1985 Samantha and her father were killed in an airplane crash. The little girl who believed that "people can get along" was gone but not forgotten. The Soviet government issued a stamp in her honor and named a diamond, a flower, a mountain, and a planet after her. Samantha's home state made a life-sized statue of Samantha and put it near the Maine state capitol in Augusta.

Samantha's mother established the Samantha Smith Foundation in October 1985 to pay for projects that teach people about peace and encourage friendships among children of all nations. Samantha made a difference and so can you.

Happy are those who strive for peace.
Matthew 5:9 TLB

HELP INSPIRE PEACEFUL BEHAVIOR.

Make friends with people you think are very different from you and enjoy the things that you have in common. Be a peacemaker.

We're Not Impressed

Liars are not believed even when they tell the truth.

———— ❋ ————

"What did you get for Christmas?" Mary Beth asked Elli when they got back to school from winter break.

"I got a sled and a jacket and a new CD player," Elli replied. "What did you get?"

"I got a telephone of my own and new boots. My family got a big-screen television. It's huge!"

Sheryl overheard their conversation and joined in. "We went to Disneyland. My grandfather has a condominium there."

"Wow, that must have been cool!" Elli said.

"What else did you do there?" Mary Beth asked.

"We went to Hollywood and Los Angeles."

Mary Beth and Elli were in awe.

Michaela walked up as the girls were talking. "Hi, how was Christmas?" she asked.

Sheryl started walking away. "Sheryl," Michaela said, "didn't I see you at the movies during vacation?"

"Uh. It must have been someone else."

"I'm sure it was you," she said as Sheryl disappeared down the hall.

"Sheryl went to California to her grandfather's condominium for Christmas; it couldn't have been her," Mary Beth said.

"Are you sure? Her grandfather lives in my grandmother's neighborhood. She said she saw Sheryl's family at his house."

The next time Elli saw Sheryl, she asked her, "Sheryl, did you really go to California?"

"No," said Sheryl. "I'm sorry I made up a story. We really stayed with Gramps because my mother is sick."

"Sheryl, you don't have to make up a story."

"I'm sorry. I guess I was trying to impress you."

"I like you just the way you really are," Elli said. "You don't have to tell a lie to impress me or anybody."

We speak the truth. We serve in the power of God.
2 Corinthians 6:7 NIRV

ALWAYS SPEAK THE TRUTH.

Your words reflect your heart. Display a heart of truth in all you do.

Today's the Day!

[When we were growing up,] we knew about problems, heard about them, saw them, even lived through some hard ones ourselves, but our community wrapped itself around us, put itself between us and the hard knocks to cushion the blows.

Stuart and Katelyn counted their savings. They wanted to give Dad a birthday party but they weren't sure they had enough money.

Mom had kept everything going—food and clothes, rides to school and sports. She bought the presents and handled the birthday parties. She cheered for all of them, no matter what. Then Mom got sick. Dad had to work, cook, take care of them, and take care of Mom too, yet he never complained. Then Mom passed away.

"How can we do this?" Stuart said. "It has to be a surprise." They knew Dad didn't even want to think about a party.

Stuart and Katelyn finally decided to ask their neighbors for help. Everybody was eager to be a part. They sent out invitations for the party. Mrs. Connally had Mom's spaghetti recipe, and Mr. Connally said he would buy and keep all the ingredients at their house. Other people also volunteered to help. The hardest part was keeping it all a secret!

On the night of the party, the guests came one by one. Everybody brought food and gifts and parked their cars on the next block. Stuart and Katelyn had made a cake just like Mom had taught them.

Everything was ready. Mr. Connally called when he saw Mr. Givens drive around the corner. All the guests were hiding. When Dad came in they shouted, "Surprise! Happy birthday!" and started singing.

Their dad took one look at Stuart and Katelyn and wrapped them in a big hug. "You're the best birthday gift I could ever want!" he said.

Remember

You changed my sorrow into dancing. You took away my rough cloth, which shows sadness, and clothed me in happiness.
Psalm 30:11 ICB

LOOK FOR JOY IN EVERY DAY.

If you are sad about something, think about how you can bring joy to someone else—then you can share the joy together.

Untangling the Web

Oh, what a tangled web we weave when first we practice to deceive!

"Did you hear what Trista did?" asked Laura. "She copied answers from Mackenzie's geography test."

"Really? That doesn't sound like something Trista would do," Madison replied. "She's smart enough to make good grades on her own."

"Well, maybe that's how she does it."

"I don't think that's true. Trista's mother is a schoolteacher. She would never let Trista get away with something like that."

"Well, that's what Mackenzie said."

I wonder if that's really true, Madison thought to herself. *Trista and Mackenzie were always competing for the best grades.*

"You should know something, Trista," Madison said. "People are saying that you copied from Mackenzie's test. Is that true?"

"That's not true at all! Who would say such a thing?" Trista was really upset. "My parents would ground me for weeks if they ever thought I cheated. What can I do? I'll tell Miss Pennison."

228

After the class left for recess, Miss Pennison said, "Mackenzie, Trista said someone told her that you were spreading a rumor that she cheated on her geography test. Did you say that?"

Mackenzie looked down at the floor. "Yes, Miss Pennison. I did. I wanted to be the best student in our class, and I thought Trista wouldn't be the best if people thought she cheated."

"Mackenzie, that was very wrong. Do you know that?"

"Yes, Ma'am. I'm sorry. Really I am."

"You need to apologize to Trista. I'm sorry, but I'll need to talk with your parents about this."

"I know," Mackenzie said, knowing she was in trouble all around. "I'm sorry. It won't happen again. I promise."

Remember

If your heart is full of bitter jealousy and selfishness, don't brag or lie to cover up the truth. That kind of wisdom doesn't come from above.
James 3:14–15 CEV

LYING NEVER PUTS YOU AHEAD.

You Can Do It!

Stand up for the truth. Question information that you think may not be true about another person.

Junior Bridesmaids

When one has not what one likes, one must like what one has.

Aunt Megan was getting married and Blythe and Kelsey were excited. They were going to be in the wedding as junior bridesmaids! This was great fun— new dresses and shoes, hair appointments, and parties. The sisters were counting the days. Aunt Megan was their favorite aunt and they wanted everything to be perfect.

On the big shopping day, Blythe and Kelsey went with Mom and Aunt Megan to pick out their dresses. Not everyone had the same idea about what their dresses should look like! Blythe wanted to wear white, and Kelsey wanted a purple dress. Aunt Megan liked a dress that was definitely not the favorite of either girl.

What were they to do? They had thought this was going to be fun—and now it wasn't. How could they make a decision?

"Blythe and Kelsey," Mom said, "come with me. We need to talk. You only have to wear the dress once. This is Aunt Megan's big day to be the star!"

"I guess it will be okay. We've never been junior bridesmaids and we wanted to look grown-up." Both Blythe and Kelsey agreed to wear the dress Aunt Megan liked. The issue was settled and the dresses were bought.

On the day of Aunt Meg's wedding, Blythe and Kelsey put on their new dresses. They were excited even if the dresses weren't exactly what they had wanted. Aunt Meg was a beautiful bride.

As the photographer took the pictures, he said to Blythe and Kelsey, "I've never seen such beautiful junior bridesmaids. I'm going to ask your parents if I can use your photo to enter the photography contest."

Blythe and Kelsey were so surprised! "That would be okay with us," Blythe said. "Will you let us know if you win?"

It's selfish and stupid to think only of yourself.
Proverbs 18:1 CEV

DON'T THINK ONLY ABOUT YOURSELF.

If you disagree with someone today, try to understand the situation as they see it and as it benefits them.

Life Is Like a Puzzle!

When God builds the puzzle, it all fits.

"Hey, here's a piece ... I think this one fits here. Well, almost," Alex said.

"Look for the pieces with a straight edge so we can frame in the border of the puzzle first. That will make it easier to fill in the rest of the pieces," Dad said.

"Now, let's sort the pieces with similar colors. They should belong in about the same place in the puzzle," Mom added.

On this cold and snowy night, the Marsden family was working on a big 2000-piece puzzle—the box showed a picture of a pizza! All the pieces looked the same, but for each spot there was only one piece that was an exact fit. That meant 1,999 pieces were wrong!

"I'm glad we have plenty of popcorn and hot chocolate," Kiersten said. "Why are puzzles so ... well, puzzling!" Alex asked.

"That's the point," Mom said. "They are challenging. The most important point to completing a puzzle is ... don't quit. We need to keep going, keep trying."

Dad added, "Every day we face puzzling situations. There are things we don't understand. There are problems that don't work out. Perhaps math is our biggest problem."

"Or grammar. It just doesn't make sense," piped up Kiersten. "Science? Forget it!"

"But, what does it take to solve a problem?" Mom asked. "Don't quit! Keep on trying. If you have a question, ask for help. Keep on seeking and you will find!"

At just that moment, Alex found a piece that fit, and the entire family gave a cheer!

Remember

"You should be strong. Don't give up, because
you will get a reward for your good work."
2 Chronicles 15:7 ICB

KEEP ON KEEPING ON!

Are you tempted to quit? Do you really want to reach the goal? If you do, then don't give up and you will find a new way to solve the problem that has you discouraged!

Follow the Leader

I cannot and will not cut my conscience to fit this year's fashions.

"Mom, I don't have anything to wear this fall to start back to school. Can I buy some new clothes?" Kristi asked. She really looked forward to starting seventh grade.

"Let's look through your closet and see what you could use."

"I really need some new jeans and a couple of T-shirts. And I need some new shoes."

"Hmm," Mom said. "Here are some jeans from last year. Are they still long enough? You've grown over the summer."

"Those are last year's style. I don't want to wear them."

"Just try them on. Let's see. Yes, they are a bit too short. We can go shopping tomorrow."

Kristi and her mother went to the mall, and Kristi found some jeans she wanted, "I like these. That's what everyone is wearing."

"You can try them on, but they look like they're cut too low. Your dad doesn't want you to wear the low-cut jeans. I bet we can find something else."

"Mom, that's what everyone is wearing—and it is seventh grade!"

"You need to consider what your father thinks. He cares about how you look and what you wear. It's important to him because you are important to him."

"I know, Mom, but ...."

"It isn't easy to go a different direction from what everyone else is doing," Mom admitted. "But I think these other jeans will look great on you. Give them a try. And besides ... why not be a style setter instead of a fashion follower."

I also want women to dress simply. They should
wear clothes that are right and proper.
1 Timothy 2:9 NIRV

DON'T BE A SLAVE TO EVERY NEW

FAD.

Develop your own sense of style and fashion. You will look your best in what looks good on you!

Special Little Brother*

From the beginning, disability taught that life could be reinvented. In fact, such an outlook was required.

When Mara was four years old, Arden was born. At first they didn't think he was going to live—he had a hole in his heart and it was scary. But he survived the surgery, all the shots, and the medicine.

Now the family was celebrating Arden's fourth birthday. It was amazing. He had been so sick and now he was well ... mostly. Actually, Arden was a special child. He was born with Down's syndrome. That meant he wasn't like most other children, but to Mara, he was extra special.

Arden was a delight to their family. They were closer because Arden needed extra help—and they all wanted to help him. It took a long time for him to learn to walk and talk. But Mara helped him to learn.

Mara also learned a lot from Arden. He was happy, he seldom cried, and he never hit Mara. He didn't throw things or yell when she played with his toys. He liked to share whatever he had. Those were good lessons for her to learn.

Mara had to slow down to play with Arden. He couldn't walk as fast, and he couldn't kick a ball very well. But he had the biggest smile whenever she played with him. He always smiled—and that made her smile too.

Even Grandma's Labrador dog liked Arden. Missy never let anyone ride on her back … except Arden when he was little. She didn't care if Arden pulled on her tail or got up on her back. Missy was always kind and gentle to Arden. Somehow she knew he was a special child too.

Mara noticed that people looked at them a little differently when Arden was with them. Mara thought perhaps it was because they wanted a special little boy like Arden too.

"Speak up for those who cannot speak for themselves. Defend the rights of all those who have nothing."
Proverbs 31:8 ICB

EVERY PERSON HAS A GIFT.

Do you know someone with a disability? Get to know him or her and spend time with this person. You will be blessed!

Me, First!

Let's not get too full of ourselves. Let's leave space for God to come into the room.

Rebecca's grandmother and grandfather were coming for a visit. When they arrived, she ran to hug them. "Grandma and Grandpa, we are going to have fun! I've made lots of plans for us."

They got an early start the next morning. "Grandma, Granddad, let's go. I'm ready to go to the aquarium!" shouted Rebecca. It was nine o'clock and she had her gear packed for the day.

"Wow! Look at this fish—and look here. Look at the eels. Let's go to the shark tank," Rebecca said on the run.

"Slow down, Rebecca, so your grandparents can see all the fish."

"I'm ready to go to the mall!" Rebecca was already on her way out of the aquarium.

The car was hot from the sun. "Let's leave the windows down so we can feel the breeze," Rebecca said.

"Rebecca, your grandparents need the air conditioning—it's too hot for them."

"Well, okay. But I want my window open."

"Rebecca, not today. It's too hot. Please close your window."

When they got to the mall, Rebecca said she needed a new swimsuit and some flip-flops. "After we get those," she said, "we'll be ready for lunch."

Rebecca picked out a swimsuit. "I'm hungry," she said. "I love pizza. Let's get a pizza!"

"Let's find a place where we can all eat, Rebecca. Your grandparents would like a sandwich rather than pizza.

"I don't want sandwiches. I want pizza!"

"Rebecca, your grandparents came to see you, not entertain you," her mom said. "It's time to go home. We'll go out again when you are ready to consider the desires of others—especially those who love you."

Think of others as better than yourselves.
Philippians 2:3 NIRV

PREFER OTHERS.

Do you want your way in everything you do? Ask God to help you think of others first!

Let
It Go

You must choose to forgive whoever has
wronged you. Forgiveness is not an emotion,
it is a decision of the will.

Donna and her brother Carl enjoyed going to summer church camp. The camp was fifty miles from home, which made them both feel very grown-up and on their own.

Their mom helped them pack their suitcases and then drove them to the camp. Donna said hi to several of her friends as she entered the girls' dorm. Soon she was unpacked and had her bed made. She and Carl gave Mom a good-bye hug and began to settle into the camp routine.

Donna went into the dorm one afternoon to change her clothes and found a wet towel on her bed. It looked like one that belonged to Sheila, who slept in the top bunk. Donna hung it on the towel rack.

The next day, Donna found Sheila's wet bathing suit on her bed. She hung that up too. One of the other girls noticed and asked, "Why don't you yell at Sheila? She's messing up your bed."

"It's okay," Donna said. "I can handle this."

Donna decided to talk to Carl.

"I think she just wants to see how you'll react," Carl said. "Let's pray for her and ask God to straighten this out." The two bowed their heads.

The next day, the unexpected happened.

"Donna, I need to talk to you," Sheila said. "I want to apologize for leaving wet things on your bed. I've been in a really bad mood, and I took it out on you."

"Are you feeling better now?" Donna asked.

"Yeah. At Bible study last night, I realized that God wants me to take all the bad stuff in my life and let him worry about it."

"That's a great idea," Donna said. "I can tell you from experience that letting him handle things really does work."

The LORD is merciful! He is kind and patient,
and his love never fails.
Psalm 103:8 CEV

PRAY FOR THOSE WHO ANGER YOU.

When Jesus was hanging on the cross, he could have yelled at the people who put him there. Instead, he said, "Father, forgive them...." That's how we should treat people who hurt us.

241

Dollars and Sense

A penny saved is a penny earned.

"Scott has the nicest things. He's got the best bicycle and the best computer games. He gets everything," complained Susie to her mom and dad. Although Susie was older than Scott, she hadn't learned how to handle money.

"Susie, you know you get more allowance than Scott because you're older and do more chores," her father said. "Scott just saves more money than you do."

"Why don't you make a budget and write down every cent you earn and every cent you spend. That will help you see where your money is going," Susie's mother suggested.

"Sounds boring. But I'll do it," Susie agreed.

"Start with this week's allowance," Father said. He showed her how to make a chart to record how much money she had, how much money she had spent, and what she had spent it on. "It's easy. Just remember to write it down."

After two days her father asked, "How's it going, Susie?"

"I only have $6 left over from my $10 allowance."

"Where did that money go?" Father asked.

"Well, I did get some pop after school. Then I bought two candy bars from the youth group that was raising money for missions. Oh, and I got a new scrunchy for my hair.

"Now that I can see where my money goes, I can make better choices. I can choose between a pop or saving for something really nice," Susie realized.

A foolish person rejects his father's correction.
But anyone who accepts correction is wise.
Proverbs 15:5 ICB

SPEND YOUR MONEY WISELY.

Save money by not spending it. Then you will have enough for what you really want.

*Take Care of Yourself

Health is better than wealth.

Betsy couldn't understand why anyone would get up on purpose at 5:30 a.m. on a Saturday—especially in the wintertime! But her dad did it every week. He put on his jogging outfit and athletic shoes and went for a three-mile run. And it wasn't just on Saturdays. He did it several times a week! He also went to the gym to lift weights.

"Dad," Betsy asked one day, "why do you do this? Don't you get tired of getting up so early? And how can you run when it's so cold? Wouldn't you rather stay in bed and sleep?"

Dad smiled at her. "Let me ask you this," he said. "When you get older, what kind of shape do you want to be in?"

"Good shape," she said.

"And how will you stay that way between now and then?" he asked.

"I guess I just won't eat too much," Betsy said.

"Diet is important," Dad agreed, "but you have to exercise too. You have to make your heart and lungs and muscles work so that they stay healthy and strong."

"But I don't like to exercise," Betsy complained.

"You need to find something you really like to do ..."

"Like playing tennis?" Betsy interrupted.

"Exactly. Or you can ride your bike, or play basketball, or swim ..."

"Or go running?" Betsy asked, making a face.

Dad said. "I know I've done something good for my body, and it also feels good to know that I had a goal to run three miles, and I did it."

"Maybe I'll be a runner like you someday, Dad," Betsy said, "but for now, I think I'll stick with tennis."

Don't you know that you yourselves are
God's temple? God's Spirit lives in you.
I Corinthians 3:16 NIRV

TAKE CARE OF YOUR BODY.

God has given us amazing bodies to use while we are living on earth. It's our job to take care of them until we get new ones in heaven!

245

Everyone Wins

Pride slays thanksgiving, but [a] humble mind is the soil out of which thanks naturally grow.

Every other weekend was such a drag. Alice's stepsister, Esther, came to visit with her father. What made it worse was that Alice and Esther were the same age. What made it impossible was that Esther got As and Alice worked hard to pull Cs.

Esther was great in most subjects, but Alice also had talents. She was a whiz at the computer and excelled at soccer. During soccer season, she lived, ate, and breathed soccer.

There was one problem, and it was a big one. If Alice didn't keep her grades up, she couldn't play soccer. She had a big English test next week, and had to pass or hang up her cleats.

"Alice," her father said, "you need to study for your English test so you can pass next week. English is Esther's best subject— maybe she can help." Then he left to pick her up for the weekend.

Things were going from bad to worse. Alice didn't want Esther to have a clue that she could use her help.

Esther and her father got home in time for dinner.

"Alice," Esther asked, "how's school going? Are you going to play soccer this year?"

"Sure I am," she answered. Alice suspected she knew what was up and she was rubbing it in.

"I'm struggling with computer class. I just don't get it … I really don't," Esther said.

Alice had an idea, "Esther, let's make a deal. I'll help you with computers if you will help me pass the English test."

"Really?" Esther asked. "Wow, that would be too cool. If you help me, I know I'll be able to figure it out."

Alice was shocked that Esther needed help. _This could work for both of us!_ she thought.

Remember

A proud attitude leads to ruin.
Proverbs 16:18 ICB

HELP IS ALWAYS AVAILABLE.

If you need help, swallow your pride and admit your need. Then look for ways for your need to be met.

Playing the Part

Happiness is not having what you want, but wanting what you have.

Posters were up all over school to announce the next big theatre production: Cinderella. The boys did not exactly line up to try out for the role of the prince, but every girl in the sixth grade wanted to be Cinderella.

For the past two years, Pamela had had big roles in the school plays. She was good at following directions and great at memorizing lines. Of course she would try out for the lead role of Cinderella, and of course she would get it.

But she didn't. When the cast list was posted, she discovered that she was cast as one of the wicked stepsisters. To make matters worse, they wanted her to wear a large fake nose as part of her costume. She'd be the laughingstock of the whole school.

"I won't do it," Pamela told her mom as they discussed the play. "I should have the lead. I'm the best actress. They said they gave the part to Marcie because she 'looks the part.' I could look the part! I could wear a blonde wig!"

"I think they gave you this other part because they needed someone who could be funny," her mom said. "Being funny is a lot harder than being serious. Not everyone can do it. You proved you could in that play you did last year. You weren't the star, but everyone was talking about what a great job you did."

"I really wanted to be Cinderella," Pamela sighed, "but I guess there's one good thing about not getting the part."

"What's that?" Mom asked.

"I won't have to pretend I'm madly in love with the guy who's playing the prince!"

Christ has given each of us special abilities—
whatever he wants us to have out of his rich storehouse of gifts.
Ephesians 4:7 TLB

DO WHAT YOU DO BEST.

God has something special for each of us. Ask him and then follow his lead. That will bring us the greatest happiness we could ever know.

The Juggling Act

It is not enough to be busy; so are the ants.
The question is: What are we busy about?

It was important to Alisha to always be there when her friends needed her. She also wanted her mom to know that she could count on her when it came to helping out around the house.

Dad knew that Alisha was always happy to help wash the car or do yard work.

Alisha was a straight-A student, involved in Girls Club, on the gymnastics team, and very involved with a children's group at church.

At the end of an especially busy week, Alisha found herself feeling grumpy. She yelled at her little brother for something silly and then locked herself in her room, where she proceeded to cry. Flopping down on her bed, she fell asleep—in the middle of the day! This was so unlike her! And when she woke up an hour later, she didn't feel like doing anything.

Mom rapped gently on Alisha's door. Still feeling grouchy, Alisha let her in.

"What's going on?" Mom asked.

"Nothing," Alisha said. "I just want to be left alone."

Mom nodded wisely. "You're out of balance," she said.

Alisha looked confused.

"You've been doing too much," Mom said. "You're worn out. You need a break. And maybe it's time to give up some activities."

Alisha couldn't think of anything she wanted to give up, but she had to admit that she was exhausted.

"Maybe I don't have to do gymnastics every day, or volunteer for so much stuff at Girls Club, or … " she giggled "help with dinner every night!"

Mom laughed.

"It's a deal. I don't want you falling asleep in the middle of a meal."

"Nope," Alisha said. "I wouldn't want to miss dessert!"

Whatever you do, in word or deed, do everything in the name of the Lord Jesus, giving thanks to God the Father through him.
Colossians 3:17 NRSV

TAKE SOME TIME OFF.

God has plenty of work for us to do, but he never asks us to do so much that we wear ourselves out. We can be thankful that we have such a great "boss."

Who's Kid Are You?

You are mine and I am yours. So be it. Amen.

"Who's kid are you?" Mom asked in a tone of voice that sounded like a cheerleader.

"I'm one of the Williams' kids!" the three children in the backseat shouted in return, also sounding like cheerleaders.

"Who is a family?"

"We're a family!" the children responded happily.

"And what do the members of a family do?"

"They love one other!" the children shouted.

"Don't ever forget it," Mom said in a normal voice. "Remember that all day long."

The family said that every morning on the way to school. One day the middle Williams' child, Torry, asked Mom, "Why do we do this every morning?"

Mom said, "Because I want you to know that family is very important. You belong to somebody who loves you and looks out for you. You have a brother and a sister who belong to you. You need to love them and look out for them too. And most of all, I want you to know that you are valuable!"

"Aw, Mom," Torry said. "You sound just like my Sunday school teacher. She says that same thing to us about God."

"You just gave me an idea!" Mom said. "We're going to add a line!"

"Who loves the Williams family, and who does the Williams family love?" Mom yelled, again using her cheerleader voice.

"God!" the three children in the backseat shouted.

"Now—never forget that," Mom said. "Remember that all day long!"

"I will make you my own people and I will be your God."
Exodus 6:7 TEV

GOD IS OUR HEAVENLY FATHER.

It is much easier to love other people when we remember that God is their Heavenly Father too. And we can all be part of His heavenly family.

On the Right Square*

I not only use all the brains I have but all I can borrow.

"You can't move your queen that way!" Craig said to his younger sister. "I told you, it can't jump over other pieces."

The game was chess, and Craig was very good at it. Teddi was not. She just couldn't seem to remember which piece was allowed to go in which direction. She tried to put her bishop on the wrong-colored squares, and she forgot that the king could move only one square at a time.

"You need to think before you move your pieces," Craig said. "I told you to write down how the pieces can move and you always try to move too fast."

Craig went on to point out some other things she was doing wrong. Teddi grew frustrated and said, "Let's stop playing for now. I'm tired."

When their dad got home from work, he saw the chessboard and suggested that he and Teddi play a game.

"No, thanks," she said. "I'm no good. Just ask Craig. I'll never be any good."

"Is that what Craig said?" Dad asked.

"No, but he keeps criticizing me."

"Is he criticizing or trying to help you learn?"

"Criticizing," Teddi insisted.

"Is he saying things that make sense?"

"Y-es," Teddi admitted.

"Maybe you're like me—you don't like to have people point out what you're doing wrong," Dad said.

"Maybe so," Teddi sighed. "I really like chess and I really want to learn."

"Then why don't you take some of Craig's advice and see what happens?" Dad asked.

"Okay," Teddi said. "I could try again tomorrow. Maybe someday soon, I'll be good enough to beat him."

Are students better than their teacher? But when they are fully trained, they will be like their teacher.

Luke 6:40 CEV

LEARN TO TAKE ADVICE.

Sometimes other people know more than we do about some things. It's smart to listen to them and learn from them.

Heavenly Manners

He who sows courtesy reaps friendship.

"Why do I always have to say please and thank you?" Lesley complained. "And especially why do I have to say it to Bryce—he's family!"

"It's part of being polite," Mom said to her two children, who seemed to be especially eager for an argument on this particular morning.

"But why do we have to be polite?" Bryce said. "Hardly anybody else is. Nobody is very polite in the mall or at the ballpark."

Mom decided this was time for a serious talk. She sat down with the two at the breakfast table and said, "First of all, good manners help people who are strangers become friends. When you are nice to someone and say words like please and thank you, you show respect to them, and in most cases, they will show respect back to you. That's the best way to build a friendship—to respect each other."

But then Mom continued, "And besides that, good manners here on earth are just practice for what we will be doing in heaven."

"We'll have to have good manners in heaven?" Bryce asked.
"Sure," Mom said. "It's one thing that never ends.
"But what for?" Lesley asked.
"Why, to greet in a kind manner all the souls we are going to pass as we walk on the golden streets of heaven!" Mom said.

Do everything possible on your part to
live in peace with everybody.
Romans 12:18 TEV

GOOD MANNERS SPREAD PEACE.

Four of the best phrases you can ever learn are "please," "thank you," "I'm sorry," and "please forgive me." Use them often!

Surprise!

If you would keep your secret from an enemy, tell it not to a friend.

Dean and Cassidy overheard their father talking to Aunt Jo on the telephone. "Wow, this is a great surprise, Jo! Liz will be so surprised to see you. I can't wait. I promise not to tell her. It will be twice as much fun to surprise her."

Father saw Cassidy standing outside the door. "Cassidy, did you hear what we were talking about?"

"Are you planning a birthday party for Mother?" she asked. "Is Aunt Jo coming?"

"Yes, Aunt Jo and I really want to keep this a surprise. It will be more fun that way. Can you keep a secret, Cassidy and Dean?"

"Sure, Dad. We want to be part of the fun for Mom."

The party was still two weeks away. Cassidy was so excited because she loved her Aunt Jo and Uncle Larry. What fun this was going to be! But it was very hard to keep from telling Mother.

"Mother," Cassidy said one morning when they were eating breakfast. "What is one thing you would like for your birthday more than anything?" she asked.

"Oh my," Mother replied. "I can't think of what it would be."

"Dad has a surprise for you—and it is something you really, really want. It starts with the letters 'J' and 'L,'" Cassidy hinted.

Mother guessed right away what it was, but she didn't let on. "Cassidy, if it's a surprise, then let's keep it that way. That's the fun of surprises!"

"Okay, Mom."

The day of the party arrived. Aunt Jo and Uncle Larry and Mom's friends were at the restaurant when Cassidy and Dean and their mom and dad showed up. "Surprise!" they all shouted.

Mom acted surprised … but Cassidy felt bad. She had broken a promise to her dad.

Remember

Those who can be trusted keep things to themselves.
Proverbs 11:13 NIRV

DON'T TELL YOUR SECRETS.

Has someone told you a secret? Don't forget—it's for your ears only!

*Conversation with God

When you have read the Bible, you will know
it is the Word of God, because you will have
found it the key to your own heart,
your own happiness, and your duty.

"Whatcha doing?" Peter asked his big sister, Hannah.

"Reading my Bible," Hannah said. She moved a pillow next to her and invited Peter to come up and sit by her. Hannah really loved her little brother, and she knew that he adored her. Even though they were five years apart in age, they had a lot of fun together.

"Are you going to be a preacher like Pastor Thomas?" Peter asked.

"No," said Hannah. "The Bible is for every person to read, even boys and girls."

"Why?" asked Peter.

"It's like having a conversation with God," Hannah said. "God wants to say something to us so he gave us the Bible."

"Does He talk to you like my talking book?" Peter asked.

Hannah smiled. Peter loved for her to read his book that had buttons to push for different animal sounds. Sometimes she wished

God would talk to her in a voice she could hear.

"No," said Hannah. "People who heard from God in their heart wrote down what God said in this book. So when I read the Bible it's like hearing what God has to say about different things."

"What does God tell you?" Peter asked.

"He tells me what's right and what's wrong. He tells me what's good and what's bad. He tells me how I should treat other people. He even tells me how I should treat my little brother!"

"He does?" Peter asked, his eyes wide with wonder. "What does He say?"

"He says that I'm supposed to love you and teach you to read the Bible for yourself," Hannah said. And then with a big grin she added, "And I think that means right now I should hug you and kiss you ten times in a row and then tickle you."

All Scripture is inspired by God and is useful for teaching the truth, rebuking error, correcting faults, and giving instruction for right living.
2 Timothy 3:16 TEV

THE BIBLE IS OUR GUIDEBOOK FOR LIFE.

If you want God's opinion on what to think, believe, feel, say, or do ... go to your Bible. It has every answer you need.

Safety in Numbers

Courage is resistance to fear, mastery of
fear, not absence of fear.

"I'm afraid of thunder," said Tiffany.

"And I'm afraid of lightning," said Helen.

Tiffany was spending the night at her good friend Helen's house. The girls were asleep until the storm began. Then the thunder woke them. It was so loud, the windows rattled.

"Wow, I've never heard thunder that loud! Did you hear the windows rattle—do you think they will break?" Tiffany cried.

"I don't think so," said Helen. "I think we'll be okay."

Just then lightning stretched across the sky and lit up the room as if it were day. "That was really scary," Helen said. The two girls pulled the bedcovers over their heads.

"Maybe if we say a prayer, we won't be afraid. Let's ask God to help us," Tiffany suggested.

"That's a good idea," said Helen, "but I hope the storm quits pretty soon."

"Dear God," Tiffany started, "thank You for making the rain and the skies and the outdoors. We know that you are bigger than the storm. You are bigger than the thunder and lightning. You are bigger than all outdoors. And you are here with us now when we are afraid. Keep us safe in this storm. Thank You. Amen."

"My father told me when I am afraid, just to say, 'God is greater.' Because God is greater than anything I am afraid of," Tiffany said after she had prayed.

"I heard a story last week about Jesus sleeping in a boat during the storm. When the disciples woke him up, he told the winds and waves to stop ... and they did!"

"Let's think about Jesus being with us. Then we won't be so afraid."

"Good night, Tiffany. I think now we can get some sleep."

The disciples were amazed. They asked, "What kind of man is this? Even the winds and the waves obey him!"
Matthew 8:27 NIRV

GOD IS GREATER!

When you are afraid, think about Jesus being with you right where you are. He is always with you and promises never to leave you.

Bargains Galore

Help others and you help yourself.

"Mom, Dad, here's an ad for a garage sale and they have a set of uneven gymnastics bars for sale! Can we go and look at them—and maybe buy them?" Bethany asked. She wanted a set of uneven bars so she could practice in her efforts to make the gymnastics team.

"We better get out early before the set is sold," Dad suggested.

"Let's go!" She put on her shoes, brushed her hair, and was ready in two minutes.

"Bring the newspaper with the address," Mom said.

"Don't forget the checkbook," Bethany said. They all got into the van and away they went.

They found the address quickly. "I think they still have it. Let's hurry!" shouted Bethany.

Dad stopped the car in front of the garage sale sign and they all got out and went into the garage to look at the uneven bars. Dad tried them out to be sure they were sturdy and strong.

Mom looked around at other items for sale. "How much is this?" she asked about a set of pots and pans.

"Fifteen dollars," said the owners.

"We should buy that for the homeless shelter. The leaders there put together packages of kitchenware and bed linens and towels so people can set up housekeeping when they get into a house or apartment. Will you take $12 for that?" she asked.

"Sure, that's a good cause," said the owner.

"How about these sheets? They look almost new. Would you take $5 for them? I'll add those to the set of pots and pans."

"What about my set of uneven bars?" asked Bethany.

"That too," replied Mom.

"This has been a good day for shopping," said Bethany. "We've found something for everyone."

When we can do good to everyone, let us do it.
Galatians 6:10 NIRV

ALWAYS BE WILLING TO HELP OTHERS!

Look for new ways to share your resources with others. What do you have? Time? Money? Energy? Whatever you have, use it for someone who needs it.

An Up Night and a Down Day

"Good night, little girls! Thank the Lord you are well! And now to go sleep!" said Miss Clavel.

"We promise we'll go to sleep so we can get up on time for school," Roxanne said as she waved good-bye to her mother. The Carpenters had to go out of town to see Granddad who was in the hospital. They had arranged for Roxanne to stay with family friends who had a daughter the same age.

The girls did their homework, then got ready for bed.

"Lights out now," Mrs. Meyer called up the stairs. "You have school tomorrow."

"Okay," Leigh called back.

The lights went out, but Leigh and Roxanne whispered and giggled in bed until they couldn't stay awake any longer.

"It's time to get ready for school, girls," Mrs. Meyer said as she knocked on the door. It couldn't be morning already! They were so tired. Roxanne hoped she wouldn't fall asleep in class. Leigh had a math quiz. She had studied for it, but she was so tired she couldn't think well.

In physical education class Roxanne played soccer. She missed a couple of easy passes, losing the ball to the other team. Her team chided her, "Hey, Roxanne, can't you see the ball?"

"Get lost! I just missed it!" she called back. She ran off the field when the game was over.

At home, Roxanne and Leigh were quiet at the dinner table. "How was your day, girls?" Mr. Meyer asked.

"Well, tomorrow will be better. It can't get much worse!" Leigh replied.

At bedtime, Mrs. Meyer went in to shut off the light in the girls' bedroom. They had to get their sleep tonight. But they didn't need to be reminded —they had already fallen asleep with the light on!

I will lie down and sleep in peace.
Psalm 4:8 NIRV

PLEASANT DREAMS ... CREATE PLEAS-
ANT DAYS.

Start your day the night before—get enough sleep to give you enough energy to do everything you need to do well and cheerfully.

Big Friends in Sad Times*

When one has a sorrow that cannot be told to anybody on earth, it must be confided in God ... for he can make our sorrows lighter, and teach us to bear them.

Molly was not quite herself. She had always been quiet, but now she seemed to stay away from anyone who tried to include her in her activities.

"Molly, are you alright?" her second grade teacher, Mrs. Mays, asked when the two were alone after school. Molly didn't race home after school with the other children when school was over.

"I'm okay," she replied. As Molly answered, Mrs. Mays saw her lip quiver.

"Can I help you?" Mrs. Mays continued.

"I'm fine. I don't need help," Molly said as she headed for the classroom door.

"Would you like to talk with Miss Sherry?" Mrs. Mays asked. Miss Sherry was the school counselor.

That was more than Molly could take, and tears started to fall. Mrs. Mays took Molly into the classroom where they could talk alone.

"Molly, is someone giving you a hard time? Is your family okay?"

With that Molly poured out her story. Her parents were getting a divorce. Her dad had moved out and her mother was very upset. Her little brother cried for their daddy.

"Molly, I'm so sorry. That is really sad and very hard. I know you love both your mother and your dad."

Molly gulped to catch her breath, "I don't want my parents to fight. But I want them to live together. Why did this happen? Did I do something wrong?"

Mrs. Mays held Molly's hands in hers. "Molly, sometimes grown-ups don't know how to get along and so they think it is better to live in different houses. You didn't do anything wrong, honey. Let's make an appointment with Miss Sherry tomorrow. You can tell her just how you feel."

Remember

The Lord is close to those whose hearts have been broken.
He saves those whose spirits have been crushed.
Psalm 34:18 NIRV

BE A GOOD LISTENER.

If you have a problem that is bigger than you can handle, tell an adult that you can trust. If you know someone else who has a big problem, encourage her to get help from someone she trusts.

More to Learn

Isn't it amazing that almost everyone has an opinion to offer about the Bible, and yet so few have studied it?

"I don't know why Dad makes us read the Bible and memorize verses every week. Nobody else in Sunday school class memorizes them," Tyrone said to his sister Taylor.

"At least not every week," Taylor said.

"I heard that!" Dad said as he walked into the room and sat down at the kitchen table with them. "Are you telling me that you don't know why I have you memorize Bible verses?"

"Not really," Tyrone said. "I know you think it's good for me, but I don't really know why it's good for me. I have three Bibles I can read."

"First," Dad explained, "you'll find when you are older that you remember what you've memorized more than you remember what you just read. I want you to remember the Bible, just like you remember the Pledge of Allegiance that you memorized. But you may not remember what you read in history class last week."

"You got that right," Taylor said.

"Second," Dad went on, "if you've memorized lots of Bible verses, you'll have a better idea about what's really in the Bible. You are going to meet people who will tell you what the Bible says but they've never read it for themselves so they don't really know what it says. Sometimes people will tell you something is in the Bible when it isn't, and sometimes they'll tell you something isn't in the Bible when it is."

"Like what?" Tyrone asked.

"Ever heard the saying 'An apple a day keeps the doctor away'?" Dad asked.

"Sure," said Taylor. "Gram says that all the time."

"Is it in the Bible?" Dad asked as he got up and walked away.

"Is it?" Taylor asked her big brother.

"I guess we have some more reading and memorizing to do," Tyrone said.

I will repeat aloud all the laws you have given.
Psalm 119:13 TEV

LEARN THE BIBLE WELL.

If you memorize one verse from the Bible every week, you'll know hundreds of verses by the time you grow up!

God Is Watching

Wisdom is seeing life from God's perspective.

"The stock market took another nosedive today ..."

"You might have noticed that it costs a lot more to fill your car's tank with gas this week ..."

"A major airline announced today that ticket prices are going up ..."

"A local computer software firm is laying off thirty percent of its employees ..."

Faith's dad watched the news and shook his head. "Things are going from bad to worse," he muttered. "We'll all wind up at the soup kitchen before too long."

Faith was horrified. She'd been to the local soup kitchen, where her mom sometimes volunteered, and she couldn't imagine having to eat all of their meals there.

"Are we really almost out of money, Daddy?" she asked, her voice shaking.

"What? No, Faith! No!" Dad said. "I'm sorry. I shouldn't have said that. I just get discouraged sometimes when I see how things are in this world."

"Are we really okay?" Faith asked.

"Yes, Faith. Come sit over here and let me explain something." Faith sat on the couch beside her dad.

"Even when things aren't going well around us—like layoffs and higher prices—we have to remember that God is still bigger than all of us, and he is in control. God is our Father, and we can trust him to take care of us."

"The way that you and Mama take care of me?" Faith asked.

"Yes," Dad said. "We want what is best for you. So does God. I'm glad you reminded me, Faith, to stop worrying about the news and start listening to God."

Depend on the Lord; trust him, and he will take care of you.
Psalm 37:5 NCV

LISTEN TO GOD.

God is well aware of everything that is happening in this world. After all, he created it! We can trust him to protect us when things seem to be going crazy.

Doing the Right Thing

What's left after all the excuses are gone is usually what's right.

"What's that mean?" Dayton asked, pointing to Michelle's bracelet.

"You've never seen a WWJD bracelet before?" Michelle said.

"No," said Dayton. "What's it mean?" Michelle suddenly remembered that Dayton had lived in South America where his parents were missionaries. "WWJD bracelets are kinda old here in the United States," Michelle said, "but I still like to wear mine. WWJD stands for 'What Would Jesus Do?'"

"Why do you wear it?" Dayton asked.

"Well," Michelle said, "sometimes I don't know what to do in certain situations, or I don't know what to say—like when Chris punched Garrett in the stomach at recess today."

"That was a pretty bad scene," Dayton replied. "I saw it from across the cafeteria. What's with those two?"

"Garrett and Chris are normally friends, but Garrett took a candy bar out of Chris' lunch sack. They were both wrong—

Garrett was wrong to take the candy bar and Chris was wrong to punch him," Michelle said.

"So what would Jesus do?" Dayton asked.

Michelle said, "I think he would have done exactly what Kip did. Kip handed Chris an even bigger candy bar from his own lunch sack and said, 'Don't be stupid. A candy bar isn't worth fighting about.'"

"You really think that's what Jesus would have done?" Dayton asked.

"Well, maybe not exactly like that, but I do think Jesus would have wanted Chris and Garrett to stay friends," Michelle said.

"I think I'd like Kip to be my friend," Dayton said.

Put all things to the test: keep what is good and avoid every kind of evil.
1 Thessalonians 5:21–22 TEV

GOD'S WAY IS THE RIGHT WAY.

Any time you wonder if you're doing the right thing ask Jesus, "Is this what You would do?"

Jump or Draw?

The real tragedy of life is not in being
limited to one talent, but in the failure to
use the one talent.

When it came to jumping rope, Tina was terrific. She loved to challenge her friends, to see who could jump rope the longest. Tina usually won the contests in gym class.

Jane was not very good at jumping rope. Somehow, her feet always got tangled up in the rope, and she was forced to sit and watch the other kids continue their jumping.

During the lunch period one day, Jane carried her tray to Tina's table and asked if she could sit down.

"Sure," Tina said.

"I wanted to tell you what a great jump roper you are," Jane said as she put the straw in her milk bottle. "I wish I could jump like you."

"It just takes practice," Tina said, biting into her sandwich.

"No, I think it takes talent," Jane said. "My mom says that God gives each of us certain talents, and that we're not all good at the same things."

"Could be," said Tina thoughtfully. "I've always been good at jumping rope."

"My mom says the important thing is to find out what your talents are and use them the way God wants you to."

"What's your talent?" Tina asked.

"I drew this picture of you," Jane said, pulling a piece of drawing paper out of her notebook.

"Wow!" exclaimed Tina. "That looks just like me! If I were you, I'd forget about jumping rope."

"I'm going to keep jumping," Jane said, "but I know that drawing is my real talent."

"Can you show me how to draw?" Tina asked. "Maybe I've got another talent I didn't even know I had."

There are different kinds of gifts .... But they all come
from the same Lord.
1 Corinthians 12:4–5 NIRV

DON'T WASTE YOUR TRUE TALENTS.

God has given everyone different gifts and talents. It's fun for us to figure out what they are! It's even more fun to use them, all for his glory.

The Big Lie

Forgiveness is a funny thing—it warms the
heart and cools the sting.

Paige and Grace were running against each another in the election for class president. For weeks, they had been putting up posters in the halls, handing out flyers at lunch, and asking for votes.

Paige thought she had a good chance of winning, so she was shocked when the votes were counted and she learned that she had received only half as many votes as Grace.

"Better luck next time," Grace said with a smirk as she went to the stage to give her acceptance speech. Paige sat in the auditorium and wondered what she could have done to convince more classmates to vote for her.

"I found out why you lost," Mae said to Paige as they ate lunch later that day. "Grace spread a rumor that you get good grades because you bribe the teacher."

Paige couldn't believe her ears!

"If I were you, I'd get even," Mae said. "Tell the principal!"

"I'll tell the principal the rumor's not true," Paige said, "but I won't say who started it. I feel sorry for Grace if she feels she had to lie to win the election. I'll tell her I know what she did, and that I forgive her. Then I'm going to pray for her. She's our class president now, and we all want her to be a good one, don't we?"

"I can't believe you're letting her off the hook like this," Mae said.

"I don't need to get revenge," Paige said. "The right thing to do is to let God work this out."

If God is on our side, who can ever be against us?
Romans 8:31 TLB

DON'T WASTE ENERGY ON ANGER.

It's hard to accept a loss when someone else has done something wrong that caused us to lose. Rather than try to get even, let God deal with the other person.

279

A New Outlook

Prejudice is the child of ignorance.

For as long as Janine could remember, the railroad track divided the town's two main neighborhoods—not by design, it had just turned out that way. The poor people lived on one side of the track. Many of them had come to the town during what people called the "dust bowl" days.

The shopkeepers and farmers who employed them lived on the other side of the tracks. They had more money and nicer homes.

Janine lived on the "good side" of the tracks, and the kids in her neighborhood regularly called the dust-bowl people "Okies" because they came from Oklahoma.

"You can't go to the party with her," Janine said to her older brother, Tim.

"Why not?" Tim said. "She's the prettiest girl in my class. One of the smartest too."

"But she's an Okie," Janine said.

"And what does that mean?" Tim asked.

"Well, her family doesn't have as much money as we do," Janine said.

"She goes to our church," Tim said. "And her mother shops at our grocery store and her father gets gasoline at our gas station."

"But she lives on the other side of the tracks," Janine said.

"Listen, Janine," Tim finally said. "I like Connie. Her folks had a hard time, but they're good people, and they're working hard to make a better life. Connie's fun and nice. As far as I'm concerned, 'Okie' stands for Outstanding Kid In Everything."

"But what will people say?" Janine said.

"It only matters what God says," Tim replied with a smile. "And by the way, Connie has a really cute brother."

Remember

There is no longer any distinction between Gentiles and Jews, circumcised and uncircumcised, barbarians, savages, slaves, and free men, but Christ is all, Christ is in all.
Colossians 3:11 TEV

GOD LOVES ALL HIS CHILDREN.

God loves people of all races, cultures, and nations—and we are to love them too.

New Chapter in Friendship

A generous action is its own reward.

Ashley loved to read. She especially loved to read mysteries. She had a favorite author who had written twenty books, and Ashley had just added the latest book to her collection. Now she had all twenty.

Ashley's best friend, Hank, who lived next door, loved the same books. He usually checked them out at the library. But there was a long waiting list for the new book, so he asked Ashley if she would loan him her copy.

"No way!" Ashley said. "I just got it, and I don't want it to get messed up."

Hank got angry and stormed home. Ashley felt bad, but she still couldn't bring herself to loan him the book.

At dinner that night, Ashley's family talked about ways to be more like Jesus.

"What was Jesus like?" Dad asked.

"He loved everybody. He forgave people. He was nice to people, and He gave His life for us," Ashley said.

"How can we copy that?" Mom asked.

"Maybe by being really generous," Ashley said, thinking about her book. "Maybe by loaning to a friend something that really means a lot to us."

After dinner Ashley knocked on Hank's door. When he opened it, she handed him her book.

"I changed my mind," she said. "I think you'll like this a lot. As soon as you finish reading it, we can talk about our favorite parts."

"Thanks!" Hank said. "I promise to take good care of it."

"I know you will," said Ashley. "I know I can trust a good friend."

Remember

The group of followers all felt the same way about everything. None of them claimed that their possessions were their own, and they shared everything they had with each other.
Acts 4:32 CEV

GENEROSITY OPENS HEARTS TO JESUS.

When we think about everything that Jesus did for us—giving up his home in heaven and coming to earth to live the way we live—that makes it easier to share what we have with others.

Appointment with God

Have some time for yourself, and some time for your God.

By the time Brenda and her mother got home from the family reunion on Saturday night, it was nearly 12 o'clock. Brenda fell asleep as soon as her head hit the pillow. She dreamed that she and her cousins were swimming in the lake and roasting marshmallows on the beach—just like they had at the reunion.

It seemed as if she'd been asleep only for a few minutes, when … BRRRING! The alarm clock signaled the time to get up for Sunday school. Brenda turned off the alarm, groaned, and rolled over. A few minutes later, her mom came in to make sure she was up.

At the breakfast table, Brenda was out of sorts. "Why can't I sleep in?" she argued. "What difference does it make if I miss Sunday school now and then?"

Brenda's mom put down her coffee cup. "Think about yesterday and how great it was to be with people you have something in common with. And your cousins have taught you some neat stuff, like how to swim. In Sunday school, you're with other kids who love Jesus. You're all learning things about him that you will carry with you for the rest of your life. If you miss a Sunday, you might miss a really important lesson that you'll need later on.

"Not only that," Mom said, with a twinkle in her eye, "but God is expecting us. We have an appointment with him every Sunday, and he'd miss us if we didn't show up."

"You mean he's looking at his watch, wondering where we are?" Brenda laughed. "I guess we'd better hurry then!"

Christ is the one who holds the building together and makes it grow into a holy temple for the Lord. And you are part of that building Christ has built as a place for God's own Spirit to live.
Ephesians 2:21–22 CEV

KEEP YOUR APPOINTMENT WITH GOD.

Church is like a once-a-week family reunion. It gives us the chance to check on each other, pray for each other, and praise and worship God, our Father, together. It's something you don't want to miss.

Waiting for a Green Light

Doing what's right isn't the problem. It's knowing what's right.

———— ✲ ————

It was five o'clock in the morning. The sun wasn't up yet, but the Taylor family was on the road, heading to Granddad's house for Thanksgiving.

Ronny, his brother, Zachary, and his sister, Eve, were barely awake in the backseat of the SUV.

"Why do we have to leave so early?" Ronny grumbled.

"Because it's an eight-hour drive to Granddad's," his mom said. "We need to be there in time for dinner."

"And don't forget," Dad said, "that we're taking the food. Granddad doesn't get around too well anymore, and since Grandma died last year, he needs someone to do the cooking for a big meal like this."

The streets were deserted at this early hour. It seemed strange to the children to be alone on what was usually a very busy road.

Dad approached an intersection and stopped as the traffic light turned red.

"Why are we stopping?" Zachary asked. "There aren't any cars or any cops. Why can't we just go?"

"Because that would be breaking the law," Dad said. "The law isn't just for times when there are other people around watching you."

"Laws protect us too," Mom said. "If we ran the red light and another car suddenly came along, we could be in an accident and get hurt."

"We should always do what's right, not what's convenient," Dad said. "That way, you always know what to do."

"Anyway, who wants to make tough decisions at five o'clock," Ronny said, yawning.

"I just made an easy one," said Zachary, leaning back in his seat. "I'm going back to sleep."

Whoever obeys the law and teaches other people
to obey the law will be great in the kingdom of heaven.
Matthew 5:19 NCV

FOLLOW THE LAW.

God wants us to do what's right, and that includes following the law—his law and the laws of our country.

Birthday Giving

The covetous person lives as if the world were made altogether for him, and not he for the world.

"Let's do something different for your birthday party this year," Mom said, as she went into Corrine's room and sat on the edge of her bed.

"What?" Corrine asked eagerly, looking up from her homework. Mom always had great ideas for parties.

"How about asking your friends to bring a gift you can take to the homeless shelter to give to the girls there."

Corrine wasn't sure she liked that idea. "All my gifts would go to homeless girls?" she asked.

Mom could tell Corrine was disappointed. "Cor," Mom said, "can you name for me the presents you got last year at your party?"

"Sure!" Corrine said. But then she started thinking, *Was that gift for Christmas or my birthday? Was that something I bought or was it given to me?*

Mom pulled out a list. She said, "I know what you received." As she read through the list of seven gifts, after she read each one she said what had happened to the gift. Four of them fell into the "never used it, read it, or played with it after the first day" category. Two of the gifts had been given to her younger sister. One gift had been lost after a week. "Wouldn't it have been better to have given all of those gifts away to children who really would have used them?" Mom said. "You have lots of things, Corrine. And with your very generous allowance and the money gifts you get from family members, you buy what you like and want to have."

"I guess you're right," Corrine said.

"A birthday is just as good a time for giving as it is for receiving," Mom said.

Corrine had never thought about it that way before.

Be satisfied with what you have.
Hebrews 13:5 TEV

FOCUS ON WHAT YOU HAVE.

Think about a person who has a big need. Think of what you have that you might give to help, encourage, or show love to that person. Then talk over with a parent the idea of giving your gift.

Choosing the Truth

Truth is not always popular, but it is always right.

"It's not really a lie," Hope said. "We are going to the mall."

"Yeah," Felicia replied, "but what you've got in mind is going to a movie that's in the theater at the mall."

"Right," said Hope. "But it is at the mall!"

"You know our parents haven't given us permission to see that movie. It's rated R, and our parents have told us we aren't allowed to see R-rated movies."

"They'll never know," Hope stressed. "Everybody says this is the greatest movie they have ever seen. Don't you want to see it?"

"I guess," Felicia said. "It'll be hard not to talk about the movie if it's that great, but if we say anything at all, our folks will pick up on that."

"You can keep your mouth shut for just once," said Felicia.

"But will they let us in? We don't exactly look seventeen."

"Speak for yourself," said Hope. "Nobody can really tell these days if a teenager is thirteen or seventeen. Act like you're seventeen and they'll think you're seventeen."

"What if somebody asks for ID?" said Felicia.

"I've never seen anybody ask for ID, have you?" Hope asked. "Are you going or not?"

Felicia thought for a minute. "Not," she said.

Hope said. "Why are you being so weird about this?"

"Well, I'm not going to say I'm at the mall when I'm at a movie. I'm not going to try to remember not to talk about a movie I'm not supposed to see. I'm not going to pretend I'm seventeen."

"Well, what do you want to do on Saturday afternoon?" Hope asked.

"Go to the mall," Felicia replied, "and shop! I've got two discount coupons and a gift certificate!"

"Why didn't you say so?" Hope smiled.

Do not lie to one another, for you have put off the
old self with its habits and have put on the new self.
Colossians 3:9–10 TEV

LIES ARE WHAT YOU FAIL TO SAY.

It is easier to tell the truth than to lie, because when you tell the truth, you don't have to remember what to say! Ask the Lord to help you be a "truth speaker."

The Great Soda Wreck

The person that loses her conscience has nothing left worth keeping.

——— ✳ ———

"Corey and Candy, where in the world did you get all that soda?"

The twins' dad had glanced up from his newspaper just in time to see his children headed toward the refrigerator with armloads of soda cans.

"It was free!" Corey responded. When Corey got as far as the table he put down his load and took a few more cans out of various pockets in his pants and jacket as his dad watched.

"Free?" asked his dad.

Candy explained as she opened the refrigerator. "There was this big wreck down on Elm Street and a delivery truck spun around. When it did, big packs of soda pop came sliding out into the street and broke open. There was soda pop EVERYWHERE! Nobody was hurt—hardly any damage to the truck or car. But everybody started picking up all the loose cans of soda."

"Did you ask the driver if you could have the soda?"

"Well, no ... not exactly."

"Then the soda wasn't free. Things taken without the owner's permission are stolen, not 'found,'" Dad said.

Candy's face went white. "No, Dad! Really! Everybody was doing it. Even the grown-ups!"

"When you get to heaven, you won't get to explain what all those other people did, just what you did."

Corey scowled for a second, then said to his Dad, "Hey, Dad, you think you can help us find out how to return these cans of soda?"

Candy quickly added, "P-l-e-a-s-e."

Dad smiled. "Let's go!"

Remember

You might see your enemy's ox or donkey wandering away.
Then you must return it to him.
Exodus 23:4 ICB

FINDERS ARE NOT ALWAYS KEEPERS.

If you find something someone lost, do your best to find the owner. If you don't know for sure what to do, ask a parent or teacher to help you figure it out.

293

Jealousy in Disguise

The person who sees himself as valuable is rarely jealous of other people who own valuable things.

"How was school today?" Mom asked Cindy as she picked her up after school.

"Terrible," said Cindy. "Sabrina noticed at lunch that I had new shoes and Cassie said, 'They sure make your feet look big.' Two girls from the next table began to look down at my feet, and then they started to laugh, but they wouldn't tell me what they were saying when I asked them what was so funny."

Mom looked down at Cindy's feet. "Aren't those the same shoes we saw in the magazine that you said were 'in' this year? And, for the record, they do not make your feet look big."

"It wasn't just that," Cindy said. "Dawn told me that this style of shoes doesn't go with my outfit, and Andrea spouted off that I shouldn't be wearing navy shoes with a gray outfit … I should be wearing black shoes. It turned out to be pick-on-Cindy's-new-shoes day."

Mom said, "I read one time about a jewelry store in New York City that put a very large flawless diamond on display—it was nearly seventy carats, which is a huge diamond. One woman saw the diamond and said she thought she saw a flaw in it. Another woman said she didn't think it was all that beautiful. Another woman said she thought it would be too vulgar to ever wear such a diamond to a party."

"Sounds like they wished they could have had it but they didn't want to admit it," said Cindy.

"Yes," said Mom, "it sure does sound like that!" She looked at Cindy and then looked down again at Cindy's new shoes.

"You shall not covet … anything that _is_ your neighbor's."
Exodus 20:17 NKJV

WE ARE VALUABLE BECAUSE GOD LOVES US.

When you choose to be happy with what God has given you, you'll find it much easier to be happy about what God gives your friends.

The Mirror

As we grow as unique persons, we learn to respect the uniqueness of others.

"Why are you frowning?" Mom asked Shara. "That's a pretty wonderful girl in the mirror."

Shara wasn't getting ready to go anywhere—she was just experimenting with a little makeup and hair clips in front of her mirror.

"I don't think there's a chance for me," Shara said with a sigh.

"A chance for what?" Mom asked.

"A chance for me ever to be pretty."

"You're darling!" Mom said.

"You're my mother and you have to say that," Shara replied. "But my nose is too big and I have too many freckles and my hair won't do anything I want it to do. And besides that, I'm too tall."

"Hmmm. Sounds just right to me," Mom said.

"M-o-m," Shara moaned. "Just admit it. I'm not pretty. I'm nice and smart and I have an okay personality. I play the flute pretty well, but I'm NOT pretty."

"Shara," Mom said, "I think you're lovely and I also think you look just like your Aunt Carolyn when she was your age—and she's a very beautiful woman. But it doesn't matter what I think. It matters what you think."

Shara was quiet. Mom continued, "God made you the way you are. He must have wanted a tall girl with freckles to love him. Your hair is just fine if you don't try to put it up. God must have wanted a tall girl with freckles who would wear her hair down. And your nose is not too big for your other features. God made just the right nose for your face."

She concluded, "Do you think God makes mistakes?"

"No," said Shara.

Mom smiled at Shara as she said, "Neither do I! Nothing about your appearance should keep you from praising God."

Remember

You created every part of me;
you put me together in my mother's womb.
Psalm 139:13 TEV

WHEN GOD MADE YOU, HE SAID, "IT
IS GOOD!"

If there's something you don't like about your appearance and you can change it, then change it. If you can't change it, thank and praise God for it. He had a good reason for making you the way you are.

The Election

The strength and happiness of a man consists in finding out the way in which God is going, and going that way too.

"Are they all blank?" Angie asked as Mick began to sort through the contents of the box.

"All blank," Mick said.

"Are you thinking what I'm thinking?" Mick said as he held up a stack of ballots.

This year the school election was handled a little differently. Yellow ballots were given to the students to vote for student body president, green ballots for vice president, blue ballots for secretary, and orange ballots for treasurer. The principal chose Angie and Mick to count the yellow ballots in a back room near his office and report their findings. There were three boxes of yellow ballots—but one of them was a box of unmarked ballots!

"We could make anybody we choose the president," Mick said.

"All we'd have to do is mark some blank ballots and substitute them for ballots that aren't marked the way we want." Angie added, "Then we could throw away the old ballots."

"We'd have to hide the old ballots in our clothes," Mick said, caught up in the idea.

"Maybe we should see who won first," Angie suggested.

"Right," Mick added as he started sorting.

Angie suddenly said, "What are we thinking, Mick! We can't do anything with those blanks!"

"Did you suddenly get a conscience?" Mick asked.

"No," said Angie. "I suddenly remembered I have one."

"You're right," Mick said.

Five minutes later Principal Brown walked in. "Did you find an extra box of blank ballots?" he asked.

"They're right here," Angie said.

"Glad you weren't tempted," Principal Brown said with a smile as he picked them up and walked out.

"We must obey God, not men."
Acts 5:29 TEV

OBEY GOD'S LAWS, EVEN IF NOBODY IS
WATCHING.

Ask God to show you what he wants you to do ... then do it.

A Shift in Plans

Diligence overcomes difficulties.

"How's the money for your orphanage fund coming?" Mom asked Joanie a few months after Joanie had pledged forty dollars to a mission orphanage her church sponsored.

"Not so good," Joanie said. "Nobody seems in the market for lemonade and chocolate chip cookies. Only one car has stopped this afternoon."

"You've got great lemonade and really good cookies," Mom said. "Maybe you need to rethink your sales plan."

"What more can I do?" Joanie said. "I've put signs everywhere I know to put them."

"Maybe you need to take your lemonade and cookies to the customer rather than have the customer come to you."

"What do you mean?" Joanie asked.

"Well, there's a softball field just three blocks away. Lots of the teams play there in the late afternoon and early evening. It's still hot at that time of day. Why not load up your brother's red wagon with your ice chest and cookies and go to the bleachers and see if anybody is interested."

"Great idea!" Joanie said. An hour later, she had made an extra jug of lemonade and had packed up two dozen more cookies.

Joanie counted out her money at bedtime. "I made more today than any day since I started," she said. "I totally ran out of lemonade and cookies. I can hardly wait until tomorrow. I have thirty-seven dollars already. Mom ... tomorrow's the day I go over the top! Thanks for the great idea."

"You know, Joanie," Mom replied, "the Lawtons—the missionaries at the orphanage—had to go where the orphans were. That's the way it is with all kinds of service. You have to go where the needs are rather than wait for the needs to come to you."

On with it, then, and finish the job! Be as eager to finish it
as you were to plan it, and do it with what you now have.
2 Corinthians 8:11 TEV

KEEP WORKING THE PLAN GOD GIVES
YOU.

If God gives you a goal, trust him also to give you a plan for reaching that goal. Ask him to give you the courage and perseverance to "work the plan" until you succeed.

The Reason

Obedience is the mother of success and is wedded to safety.

"Oops," Becca said as she stopped suddenly.

"Yeah," Brad added under his breath.

The two had been picking berries all morning. Grandpa had taught them how to pick the biggest, ripest berries and how to protect themselves from the thorns on the bushes. It was hot, hard work, but the thought of the pies Grandma was going to bake kept them going!

Grandpa had already taken their full pails back to the house and they had been working to fill two more pails by noon. Just before he left, Grandpa had told them not to cross the fence.

"Grandpa probably didn't know about those berry bushes," Becca had said as she looked at several bushes filled with ripe berries just beyond the fence.

"They aren't very far across the fence," Brad said. "We could get over there and back before anybody knew."

So, the two of them had climbed the fence and picked berries, not noticing that they hadn't stopped picking berries in the bushes closest to the fence but had moved on into the pasture from one clump of bushes to another.

"Maybe he hasn't seen us," Becca whispered as she took a step backward. Brad also began to walk backwards and then, as the huge bull took aim and began to lope toward them, they both turned and ran as fast as they could. They barely made it to the fence in time. Their pails went flying as they climbed the fence, scattering berries in a large circle.

Becca and Brad scrambled to pick up the berries just as Grandpa arrived. "I see you two met Reason," Grandpa said.

"Reason?" Becca asked.

"Yep," Grandpa said. "That's the name of that old bull."

Brad asked, "Why is he named Reason?"

Grandpa grinned. "He's the reason not to climb over that fence!"

Remember

Children, it is your Christian duty to obey your parents,
for this is the right thing to do.
Ephesians 6:1 TEV

OBEDIENCE KEEPS YOU OUT OF HARM'S WAY.

You Can Do It!

Obeying may not be easy, and it may not always be fun—but it is always right. Ask God to help you.

Psalms for Chores

Every Christian sings a slightly different song, but they will all make up a wonderful symphony in the throne room of heaven.

"Guess what I learned in Sunday school class this morning?" Kenna asked her Mom.

"What?"

"I learned the word 'psalm' means song!" Kenna said excitedly. "The Psalms in the Bible are like a songbook. Our teacher said it was like a hymnal put into the middle of the Bible."

"Right," Mom agreed.

"And we did a little experiment," Kenna continued. "The teacher asked us to open our Bibles by just letting them fall open naturally. She said most of the time if a person did that, the Bible would open up in the middle to the Psalms. We tried it and it worked. Everybody's Bible opened up to a Psalm."

"I can see how that would be true, too!" Mom said.

"The teacher said most of the Psalms are about giving praise to God. She said praise belongs right in the middle of our lives just like the Psalms are right in the middle of the Bible."

"You had a great Sunday school lesson today!" Mom said. "Do you suppose we should have a time of praise in our home right in the middle of every day this summer?"

"Yes!" Kenna said. Then she thought for a minute. "How can we do that?"

"We might start by playing some praise music loud enough to fill the whole house, and then everybody could sing along while they do their chores."

"We'd be like a choir doing chores!" Kenna said. "That could make doing chores a lot more fun, especially if you'd sing harmony, Mom."

"I think I could manage that," she said. "Who knows … it might add to the harmony of our family too!"

It is good to sing praise to our God;
it is pleasant and right to praise him.
Psalm 147:1 TEV

GOD ENJOYS YOUR PRAISE.

You don't have to wait for a "praise and worship service" to praise God. You can praise him right NOW with a song you make up!

✸The Power of Compliments ✸

I will speak ill of no man, not even in the matter of truth, but rather excuse the faults I hear, and, upon proper occasions, speak all the good I know of everybody.

"I just don't get her," Gina said to her friend Audra. She was talking about Emma, a new girl in their school that year.

"She just moved here, and she has tons of friends," Audra said. "She's not all that pretty, and she doesn't dress well. But suddenly she's one of the most popular girls in school!"

"And not just with the girls," Gina added. "The boys like her too."

Lou, another of their friends sitting at the lunch table, said, "I know why."

"Why?" Gina and Audra said in unison.

"When Emma hit this school, she began to pass out compliments. She even gave me a couple of compliments, so I know she must have given you some."

"Yeah, but nobody pays attention to compliments," Audra said. "Everybody is always saying nice things when they don't really mean what they're saying. They just say nice things to get you to like them and it doesn't work."

"But that's the difference!" Lou said. "Emma really means what she says. First of all, she says things that are true. One day she told me she really liked my lipstick. I was wearing a great new color I had just bought. On another day she told me she thought my sweater was perfect for me because it matched the color of my eyes ... she was right! She said what was true."

Lou continued, "She took the time to notice what was good and then she said what was good ... and she meant it."

"Gramma used to say that honey attracts bees better than vinegar does. I think Emma's grandmother must have told her that too," Gina said.

"Well, it sure works," said Audra. "I'm going to try it."

Do not criticize one another, my friends.
James 4:11 TEV

BE GENEROUS WITH COMPLIMENTS.

One of the best ways to make new friends—and keep old friends—is to find something nice to say to or about a person every day.

The Recital

What a difference it would make in the world if every believer were to give himself with his whole heart to live for his fellow men!

"We're going to have a recital," Mom said.

"Who for?" Lizzy asked. Her brother, Cliff, and sister, Jessie, added, "Dad doesn't count!"

The three Harper children were homeschooled. Mom had been a second-grade teacher and also taught music. She had taught Lizzy, Cliff, and Jessie to read music, play the piano, and sing. Lizzy was learning the flute, Cliff the clarinet, and Jessie the violin. At times, the house sounded like an orchestra tuning up with each of them practicing in a different room, but Mom didn't seem to mind. She wore headphones and listened to CDs!

Mom said. "You worry about your music, and I'll worry about the audience."

On the day of the recital, Mom told each of the children to dress up in their best church clothes and be ready to leave at two o'clock. "Where are we going?" asked Cliff.

"It's a surprise," Mom said. They finally arrived at a building that looked like an apartment house. "Retirement Living," Jessie said, reading the sign. "Is our recital here?"

"Yes!" Mom said. "The people who live here are older. Some of them were musicians when they were young."

The people in the retirement home clapped loudly and tapped their toes during some of their songs, but it was when they started to sing what the children called "Grandma's songs" that the people really began to smile. It seems they knew most of Grandma's songs! One man even got up out of his wheelchair to dance.

"Recitals are fun," Lizzy said on the way home.

"Yeah," added Jessie, "but only when you get your mind off being scared and watch how much fun the audience is having."

"That's true for most things in life," Mom said.

No one has ever seen God, but if we love one another, God lives in union with us, and his love is made perfect in us.
1 John 4:12 TEV

BE LIKE GOD AND SHOW LOVE TO
OTHERS.

You have much to share with others—a hug, a smile, or a song. Ask God to show you what you should share with someone today.

One More Shirt

When you get to the end of your rope, tie a knot and hang on.

"I don't know why anybody ever made all-cotton shirts, anyway. They are impossible to iron!" Camilla complained.

"I don't know why anybody made anything that needs an iron, period!" chimed in her twin sister, Carita.

The two girls were helping their mother at the church. Three large boxes of clothes had come in from two families in which an elderly grandpa had died. In the boxes were lots of shirts, some of them almost new. All of the shirts, however, needed to be ironed before they could be put out for sale in the church's secondhand clothing store. Since Camilla and Carita had learned to iron when they were young girls, their mother volunteered their help while she sorted the shirts, sewed on buttons that were loose, and took care of spots on some of the shirts.

"Just seven more shirts," Mom said.

"I just don't think I can do another one, Mom," Camilla said. "I'm so tired of ironing I'm about to fall over."

"Me, too," added Carita.

"I've got an iron going on this third board," Mom said. "I'll help you. Let's do these last shirts as if we are ironing shirts for Jesus to wear for one entire week."

The two girls and their mother talked nonstop about where they thought Jesus might wear each of the shirts they were ironing … and before they knew it, the job was done.

"Those last shirts were the most fun to iron," Carita said.

"I agree," said Camilla. "I'm just glad you didn't ask us to iron shirts for Jesus to wear for a month!"

Work hard and do not be lazy.
Serve the Lord with a heart full of devotion.
Romans 12:11 TEV

STICK WITH EVERY JOB UNTIL IT
IS DONE.

Ask God to help you complete every job you start. Ask him to help you do a good job all the way to the finish line.

The Decision

"Decisions, decisions, decisions," Jan said.

Jan had spent all afternoon sorting through things in the basement and attic with her father. They were creating one pile of things to throw away, one pile to give away, and one pile to keep and rebox.

"There's really only one decision that matters though," Dad said.

"What's that?"

"In the long run, honey, the only decision that really counts is the decision we each make about Jesus. What do we do with him? Do we accept him or reject him as our Savior?"

Jan was quiet. She'd been hearing a lot about Jesus in the last few weeks. It wasn't as if she had never been to church or Sunday school or heard about Jesus before. She knew lots of Bible stories about Jesus. It was just that lately she seemed to really be hearing what people were saying about him.

That night when she was alone in her room she thought, *I've never really made a decision about Jesus. I've never really asked him to forgive me and come live in my heart. I think tonight's the night!*

She prayed, "Dear God, I want to make a decision about Jesus right now. I believe he died on the cross for me, and I accept him as my Savior. Please, Jesus, come live in my heart and help me to follow you all my life. Amen."

Tomorrow morning I'll tell Mom and Dad what I prayed tonight, she thought. *But for right now, it feels good just to feel so clean inside.* And with that, she went to sleep. It was one of the most peaceful nights of sleep she had ever had.

For God loved the world so much that he gave his only Son, so that everyone who believes in him may ... have eternal life.
John 3:16 TEV

MAKE THE BEST DECISION.

If you have never accepted Jesus as your Savior, you can do it today! Just pray the same prayer that Jan prayed and mean it in your heart.

I N D E X

ACKNOWLEDGMENTS

Samuel Taylor Coleridge (8), Robert Browning (10), Helen Keller (12, 184), Ken Blanchard (14), Anonymous (16, 18, 34, 40, 48, 50, 54, 68, 98, 114, 118, 122, 128, 146, 154, 184, 190, 200, 204, 206, 208, 232, 276, 290, 294, 304, 312), Chinese Proverb (20, 92), Gloria Copeland (22), John Chrystom (24), Dutch Proverb (26), Thomas Merton (28), Walter Kiechel III (30), St. Francis of Assisi (32), Leo Tolsoy (36), E. B. White (38), Thomas Morell (42), Victor Hugo (44), June Kuramoto (46), Earvin "Magic" Johnson (52), George H. Lorimer (56), Billy Graham (58), Jonathan Edwards (60), Ian Percy (62), John Cassis (64), Mary Francis Shura (66), Hudson Taylor (70), Theodore Roosevelt (72), Henry Ford (74), C. H. Spurgeon (76), Horace Mann (78), Jimmy Carter (80), David E. Lilienthal (82), Marcus Aurelius (84), John Wayne (86), Winston Churchill (88), Isaac Bashevis Singer (90), William Shakespeare (94), The Bible Friend (96), William Arthur Ward (100, 278), James Michener (102), Frances J. Roberts (104), F. B. Meyer (106), Jack London (108), David O. McKay (110), Victor Hugo (112), Izaak Walton (116), John Stamos (120), John Dryden (124), Iron Eagle (126), Charlotte Lopez (130), William Temple (132), Carl Sandburg (134), Jewish Proverb (136), Horace (138), Debbi Field (140), Anne Frank (142), Henry Parry Liddon (144), Jean De La Bruyère (148), George MacDonald (150), Joan W. Blos (152), Paula Fox (156), Corrie ten Boom (158), Williams McKinley (160), Margaret Sangster (162), Dave Thomas (164), Legouve Pere (166), Pearl Bailey (168), Margaret Thatcher (170), William Penn (172),

Charles Swindoll (174), E. Stanley Jones (176), Horace Bushnell (178), Horace Bushnell (180), Ilene Cooper (182), Ralph Waldo Emerson (188), George Bush (192), Heywood Hale Broun (194), Benjamin Disraeli (196), Robert Louis Stevenson (198), Cecil Frances Alexander (202), John Kenneth Galbraith (208), Abraham Lincoln (210), Dwight D. Eisenhower (212), Miguel De Cervantes (214), Francis Bacon (216), Bernard Meltzer (218), Bibesco (220), Elbert Hubbard (222), Aesop (224), Eloise Greenfield and Lessie Jones Little (226), Sir Walter Scott (228), French Proverb (230), Lillian Hellman (234), John Hockenberry (236), Quincy Jones (238), Erwin Lutzer (240), English Proverb (242, 244), Henry Ward Beecher (246, 298), Rabbi Hyman Schachtel (248), Henry David Thoreau (250), John Wesley (252), Woodrow Wilson (254, 260), St. Basil (256), Benjamin Franklin (258, 300, 306), Mark Twain (262), Dave Dinwiddie (264), Ludwig Bemelmans (266), Johanna Spyri (268), R. C. Sproul (270), Bill Gothard (272), Edgar W. Work (276), William Hazlitt (280), William Walsh (282), Arabian Proverb (284), Lyndon B. Johnson (286), Robert South (288), Izaak Walton (292), Robert H. Schuller (296), Aeschylus (302), Andrew Murray (308), Franklin Delano Roosevelt (310).

REFERENCES

Scripture quotations marked CEV are taken from the *Contemporary English Version* © 1995 by American Bible Society. Used by permission.

Scripture quotations marked ICB are taken from the *International Children's Bible, New Century Version,* copyright © 1986, 1988 by Word Publishing, a division of Thomas Nelson, Inc. Used by permission.

Scripture quotations marked NASB are taken from the *New American Standard Bible,* © Copyright 1960, 1995 by The Lockman Foundation. Used by permission.

Scripture quotations marked NCV are taken from the New Century Version. Copyright © 1987, 1988, 1991 by Word Publishing, a division of Thomas Nelson, Inc. Used by permission.

Scripture quotations marked NIRV are taken from the *Holy Bible, New International Reader's Version.* Copyright 1994, 1996 by International Bible Society. Used by permission of Zondervan. All rights reserved.

Scripture quotations marked NIV are taken from the *Holy Bible, New International Version*®. *NIV*® Copyright © 1973, 1978, 1984 by International Bible Society. Used by permission of Zondervan. All rights reserved.

Scripture quotations marked NKJV are taken from the New King James Version. Copyright © 1982 by Thomas Nelson, Inc. Used by permission. All rights reserved.

Scripture quotations marked NRSV are taken from the New Revised Standard Version Bible, copyright 1989, Division of Christian Education of the National Council of Churches of Christ in the United States of America. Used by permission. All rights reserved.

Scripture quotations marked TEV are taken from the *Today's English Version—Second Edition* © 1992 by American Bible Society. Used by permission.

Scripture quotations marked TLB are taken from *The Living Bible,* © 1971, Tyndale House Publishers, Inc., Wheaton, Illinois 60189. Used by permission.